GUATEMALA TRAVEL GUIDE 2024 EDITION

Table of Contents

4. Top Destinations

- Antigua Guatemala

- Guatemala City

- Lake Atitlán

- Tikal National Park

- Quetzaltenango (Xela)

- Semuc Champey

- Livingston and Rio Dulce

- Pacific Coast Beaches

5. Cuisine

- Cuisine and Street Food

Conclusion

NOTE:

Embark upon an unparalleled journey as you immerse yourself in the very essence of this Guatemala travel guide. Crafted not only to inform but to spark your imagination, nurture your creativity, and awaken the adventurer within you, this guide extends an invitation to step into a realm of exploration that is distinctly your own. Departing from the ordinary, you won't find accompanying images within these pages. Our firm belief rests in the idea that the true beauty of every discovery is most vividly experienced firsthand, untainted by visual interpretations or preconceived notions.

Picture every monument, each destination, and even the hidden corners of Guatemala as exquisite surprises, patiently awaiting the moment to captivate and astonish you when you find yourself standing before them. We are steadfast in our commitment to preserving the thrill of that initial gaze, the sheer wonder that accompanies the revelation of something new. With this guide in hand, you stand on the precipice of an extraordinary voyage where curiosity is your sole mode of transportation, and this guide serves as your unwavering companion. Set aside any preconceived notions and allow yourself to be transported into an authentic Guatemala of revelations—the enchantment of your adventure begins right here. However, keep in mind that the most enchanting images will be the ones etched by your own eyes and treasured within your heart.

In stark contrast to conventional guidebooks, this volume intentionally omits intricate maps. The reason, you may ask? We ardently believe that the most extraordinary discoveries unfurl when you let yourself lose track, allowing the very essence of each place to guide you while embracing the uncertainty of the path. Bid farewell to predetermined itineraries and meticulously laid out routes, for our aim is to empower you to navigate Guatemala in your very own way, unburdened by boundaries. Allow yourself to be carried by the currents of exploration, uncovering hidden gems that remain elusive on conventional maps. Summon the courage to embrace the unknown, trusting your instincts as you boldly venture forth, prepared to be pleasantly surprised—because the magic of your journey starts now, in a realm where maps are nonexistent, and the paths unfold with each step. The most extraordinary adventures await within the uncharted folds of the unfamiliar.

Section 1: Introduction to Guatemala

Welcome to Guatemala

Nestled in the heart of Central America, Guatemala is a country that captivates visitors with its rich cultural heritage, stunning natural landscapes, and vibrant local traditions. As you set foot in this land of ancient Mayan ruins, colonial architecture, and lush rainforests, you'll be greeted by a tapestry of experiences that promises to leave an indelible mark on your journey.

Guatemala's geography is as diverse as its culture. From the towering volcanoes that dominate the skyline to the pristine beaches lining its coasts, the country's landscapes offer a breathtaking array of beauty. In the western highlands, picturesque villages are nestled among rolling hills, providing a glimpse into indigenous life and traditions. The central region is home to the bustling capital city, Guatemala City, with its mix of modernity and history. To the north, the lush jungles of Petén house the iconic ruins of Tikal, a testament to the ancient Mayan civilization.

One of Guatemala's most enchanting aspects is its cultural richness. The country is a melting pot of indigenous and colonial influences, creating a tapestry of traditions, languages, and artistry. You'll find that each town and village has its own unique character, from the cobbled streets of Antigua, a UNESCO World Heritage site, to the indigenous markets of Chichicastenango, where vibrant textiles and handicrafts showcase the artisanal talents of the local communities.

Guatemala's ties to the ancient Mayan civilization are deeply woven into its identity. The ruins of Tikal, surrounded by the verdant expanse of the jungle, stand as a testament to the architectural and astronomical prowess of the Mayans. Exploring these ruins is a journey back in time, as you traverse plazas, temples, and palaces that once thrived with a flourishing civilization.

Embarking on a culinary journey in Guatemala is a treat for the senses. Traditional dishes like tamales, made from corn dough and filled with various ingredients, and pepián, a hearty stew bursting with flavors, offer a taste of the country's heritage. Street markets brim with the aromas of fresh produce, spices, and local delicacies, while bustling food stalls offer an authentic immersion into Guatemalan gastronomy.

Nature enthusiasts will find themselves in paradise in Guatemala. The country's landscapes range from mist-covered cloud forests to crystal-clear lakes framed by volcanoes. Lake Atitlán, surrounded by quaint villages, is a tranquil haven for relaxation, water sports, and cultural encounters. Adventurous souls can trek through dense jungles, marvel at cascading waterfalls, and even hike up to the summits of active volcanoes for unparalleled views.

Guatemalans are known for their warm and welcoming nature. The genuine smiles and friendly gestures of the locals make travelers feel like they are part of the community. Whether you're participating in a local festival, chatting with artisans, or simply wandering through the streets, you'll be met with open arms and a sense of belonging.

While Guatemala embraces progress and modernity, it is deeply committed to preserving its cultural heritage. Indigenous languages and customs continue to thrive, with many communities maintaining age-old traditions that have been passed down through generations. By engaging with these traditions respectfully, visitors can contribute to the preservation of Guatemala's rich cultural tapestry.

As you embark on your journey through Guatemala, prepare to be enchanted by the mosaic of experiences that await you. Whether you're exploring ancient ruins, immersing yourself in vibrant markets, or simply soaking in the natural beauty, Guatemala promises a travel experience that is both enriching and unforgettable. Welcome to a land where the past and present intertwine, inviting you to become a part of its story.

Brief Overview of Guatemala

Nestled in the heart of Central America, Guatemala is a country of captivating contrasts and cultural richness. Bordered by Mexico to the north, Belize to the east, Honduras to the southeast, and El Salvador to the south, Guatemala boasts a diverse landscape that ranges from lush rainforests to towering volcanoes, and from bustling cities to serene lakeshores. This brief overview aims to provide a snapshot of Guatemala's history, geography, culture, economy, and more, offering a glimpse into the multifaceted tapestry that makes up this enchanting nation.

The history of Guatemala stretches back thousands of years, with its earliest chapters intertwined with the rise and fall of the Mayan civilization. The ruins of ancient Mayan cities, such as Tikal and El Mirador, stand as testament to the advanced architecture, astronomy, and societal structures of this once-flourishing culture. Following the decline of the Mayans, the

Spanish conquest in the 16th century marked the beginning of colonial rule. This period left an indelible mark on Guatemala, shaping its language, religion, and cultural fusion.

Guatemala's geography is as varied as its history. The country's terrain is characterized by towering volcanoes, fertile valleys, dense jungles, and highland plateaus. The Pacific coastline extends along the south, while the Caribbean Sea brushes its eastern shores. The central highlands, with their cool climate and breathtaking vistas, have long been home to both indigenous communities and colonial cities. From the active Pacaya Volcano to the serene Lake Atitlán, the natural wonders of Guatemala provide a canvas for both relaxation and adventure.

Guatemala is a melting pot of cultures, with indigenous traditions blending harmoniously with Spanish colonial heritage. Over 20 distinct indigenous groups, each with their own languages, rituals, and artistry, coexist within the country. This diversity is celebrated in vibrant festivals, colorful textiles, and intricate handicrafts that are emblematic of the cultural richness present in everyday life.

In the modern era, Guatemala has faced a series of challenges, including political unrest, civil conflicts, and economic disparities. The country's civil war, which lasted for several decades and ended in 1996, had a profound impact on its society and infrastructure. Despite these challenges, Guatemala is striving to create a brighter future, with efforts toward social development, economic growth, and human rights.

Agriculture has historically been the backbone of Guatemala's economy, with coffee, bananas, and sugar being major exports. In recent years, the country has also embraced tourism as a significant economic driver. The allure of ancient ruins, vibrant markets, and natural beauty has drawn travelers seeking both cultural immersion and outdoor exploration.

Guatemalan cuisine is a reflection of its diverse heritage, blending indigenous ingredients and flavors with Spanish influences. Traditional dishes such as tamales, tortillas, and chiles rellenos offer a taste of the country's culinary soul. Street food stalls, markets, and local eateries are ideal places to savor the authenticity of Guatemalan flavors.

While Guatemala is rich in cultural and natural resources, it grapples with contemporary challenges including poverty, inequality, and environmental concerns. Efforts are being made to address these issues through sustainable tourism practices, community-based initiatives, and the promotion of responsible travel.

Guatemala's allure lies in its ability to transport visitors through time and space, from ancient Mayan ruins to colonial cities and beyond. Its intricate tapestry of history, culture, and geography creates an environment that beckons exploration and discovery. Whether you're drawn to the mystique of Tikal's pyramids, the cobblestone streets of Antigua, or the warmth of the local communities, Guatemala offers an immersive experience that promises to leave an enduring impression. This brief overview scratches the surface of a country where each corner has a story to tell, waiting to be discovered by those who venture within its borders.

Cultural Background of Guatemala

Deeply rooted in indigenous traditions and shaped by centuries of historical influences, Guatemala's cultural background is a vibrant tapestry that weaves together the threads of its Mayan heritage, colonial history, diverse ethnic groups, languages, art, and spirituality. This intricate fusion of elements has created a unique cultural landscape that defines the identity of the Guatemalan people and shapes the experiences of those who visit this enchanting country.

At the heart of Guatemala's cultural background lies its ancient Mayan legacy. Long before the Spanish conquest, the region now known as Guatemala was home to the thriving Mayan civilization. The Maya's architectural marvels, complex social structures, and advancements in astronomy continue to captivate historians and archaeologists. From the towering pyramids of Tikal to the intricate stelae of Copán, these remnants of a rich past provide glimpses into the spiritual, intellectual, and artistic achievements of this ancient culture.

The Spanish conquest of Guatemala in the 16th century introduced a new layer to the country's cultural fabric. The colonial era left an indelible mark on the land, language, religion, and architecture of the region. Colonial cities like Antigua, with its cobblestone streets, ornate churches, and grand plazas, stand as living testaments to this period. The fusion of indigenous and Spanish influences is most evident in the blending of Catholic practices with ancient Mayan rituals, resulting in unique syncretic traditions.

The cultural diversity of Guatemala is enriched by over 20 distinct indigenous groups, each with its own languages, customs, and beliefs. The Maya, Kaqchikel, K'iche', and Q'eqchi' are just a few of these ethnic groups that contribute to the tapestry of Guatemalan identity. While Spanish is the official language, many indigenous languages continue to be spoken, preserving the linguistic heritage of generations past.

One of the most visually striking aspects of Guatemalan culture is its intricate textiles and handicrafts. Woven fabrics, adorned with vibrant patterns and colors, serve as a means of cultural expression and identity. Each region and community has its own unique weaving techniques and designs, often passed down through generations. From the iconic huipiles worn by women to the elaborately crafted masks used in traditional dances, these artistic creations reflect the stories, myths, and beliefs of the Guatemalan people.

Guatemala's spirituality is a complex blend of indigenous beliefs and Catholicism, a result of the syncretism that emerged during the colonial period. Many ancient rituals and ceremonies continue to be practiced alongside Christian traditions. Festivals, processions, and ceremonies are important markers of Guatemalan life, bringing communities together to celebrate, honor saints, and pay homage to their ancestors.

The culinary landscape of Guatemala is a testament to its multicultural heritage. Traditional dishes reflect a blend of indigenous ingredients and Spanish influences, resulting in a diverse array of flavors and textures. Corn, beans, chiles, and native vegetables are staples in Guatemalan cuisine, forming the basis of dishes such as tamales, pepián (a rich stew), and atol (a hot, thick beverage). Street markets offer a sensory feast, with the aroma of freshly cooked foods and the colorful display of fruits and vegetables.

Artistry in Guatemala extends beyond textiles to encompass a wide range of mediums, including painting, sculpture, and music. Indigenous artists draw inspiration from their cultural heritage to create contemporary works that honor tradition while embracing innovation. The marimba, a wooden xylophone-like instrument, holds a special place in Guatemalan music and is often associated with festive celebrations.

While Guatemala's cultural background is rich and diverse, it also faces challenges. Economic disparities, preservation of indigenous languages, and cultural heritage protection are ongoing concerns. Efforts by local communities, NGOs, and governmental initiatives are aimed at safeguarding traditions, supporting artisans, and ensuring that future generations continue to carry the torch of cultural pride.

Guatemala's cultural background is a mosaic of history, tradition, and innovation that reflects the depth of its people's experiences. From the ancient wisdom of the Mayans to the colonial legacies and the vibrant expressions of contemporary life, Guatemala's cultural tapestry is a testament to resilience, adaptation, and a deep connection to the land. As travelers immerse themselves in the country's traditions, arts, and way of life, they embark on a journey that transcends time, offering a window into a world shaped by the interplay of ancient roots and modern influences.

Section 2: Planning Your Trip

Best Time to Visit Guatemala: Navigating Seasons and Experiences

Choosing the right time to visit Guatemala is crucial for ensuring an optimal travel experience that aligns with your interests and preferences. The country's diverse landscapes, cultural festivities, and outdoor activities vary throughout the year, making it important to consider the climate, local events, and your own travel goals when planning your journey. This exploration of the best times to visit Guatemala will provide insights into the country's different seasons and the unique opportunities they offer to travelers.

Dry Season: November to April

The dry season, spanning from November to April, is often considered the best time to visit Guatemala. During these months, the weather is typically more predictable, with lower chances of rain. This makes it an ideal time for outdoor activities, such as hiking, trekking, and exploring archaeological sites. The dry season also coincides with the peak tourist season, as travelers flock to Guatemala to take advantage of the pleasant weather and festive atmosphere.

For those interested in exploring the country's highland regions, such as Antigua and Lake Atitlán, the dry season is particularly favorable. The clear skies and mild temperatures provide an optimal backdrop for exploring cobblestone streets, relaxing by the lake, and immersing yourself in local culture.

The dry season also coincides with some of Guatemala's most vibrant festivals and celebrations. Semana Santa, the Holy Week leading up to Easter, is a particularly significant event in Guatemala. Antigua, in particular, comes alive with elaborate processions, street carpets made of colored sawdust, and religious ceremonies that provide an immersive cultural experience.

Wet Season: May to October

The wet season, from May to October, is characterized by higher rainfall and occasional tropical downpours. While this might deter some travelers, the wet season has its own unique charm and benefits for those who don't mind occasional rain showers.

The wet season brings lush, green landscapes to Guatemala, transforming the countryside into a verdant paradise. The flora flourishes, and the countryside is dotted with colorful blooms. Additionally, the wet season sees fewer tourists compared to the dry season, which means you can enjoy a more peaceful and authentic experience away from the crowds.

For nature enthusiasts and adventurers, the wet season presents an excellent opportunity to explore Guatemala's rainforests and cloud forests. The rain brings life to the ecosystems, and the cooler temperatures make jungle hikes and wildlife spotting more comfortable.

Another advantage of visiting during the wet season is that prices for accommodations and tours tend to be lower compared to the peak tourist months. This can be especially appealing for budget-conscious travelers who want to make the most of their travel funds.

Choosing the Right Time for You

Ultimately, the best time to visit Guatemala depends on your personal preferences and travel goals. If you're looking for the sunniest weather and want to experience cultural festivities, the dry season is your best bet. On the other hand, if you're a nature lover who enjoys a more tranquil atmosphere and doesn't mind a bit of rain, the wet season can offer a unique and rewarding experience.

Whether you choose to visit during the dry season or embrace the lush beauty of the wet season, Guatemala has something to offer year-round. By understanding the country's seasons, weather patterns, and the experiences they bring, you can make an informed decision that aligns with your interests and allows you to fully embrace the magic that Guatemala has to offer.

Entry Requirements and Visa Information for Traveling to Guatemala

Before embarking on your journey to Guatemala, it's essential to understand the entry requirements and visa information that apply to your specific situation. Navigating the regulations for entry, stay, and departure will ensure a smooth and hassle-free travel experience. This comprehensive guide provides insights into the various entry requirements, visa options, and practical considerations for travelers planning a visit to this captivating Central American nation.

Tourist Visa Exemptions

Guatemala offers visa exemptions to citizens of several countries for short stays. Travelers from countries within the European Union, the United States, Canada, Australia, and many other nations typically do not require a visa for stays of up to 90 days for tourism purposes. However, it's essential to check with the Guatemalan consulate or embassy in your home country to confirm the current visa regulations before your trip.

Passport Requirements

To enter Guatemala, a valid passport is a must for travelers from visa-exempt countries. Ensure that your passport is valid for at least six months from your planned date of entry to avoid any complications upon arrival. It's advisable to carry a photocopy of your passport's main page and any relevant entry stamps or visas in case of loss or emergency.

Length of Stay

As previously mentioned, visitors from many countries can stay in Guatemala for up to 90 days without a visa. If you plan to stay longer than the visa-free period, you must seek an extension from the Guatemalan immigration authorities. Extensions are usually granted in 30-day increments, and it's essential to apply for an extension before your initial 90-day period expires to avoid potential legal issues.

Entry through Land Borders

Travelers entering Guatemala through land borders, such as from Mexico, Belize, El Salvador, or Honduras, should be aware of specific border crossing regulations. While many borders offer visa-on-arrival services for tourists, it's recommended to carry U.S. dollars in cash for the visa fee, as credit card facilities may not always be available.

Temporary Residency and Work Visas

If you plan to stay in Guatemala for longer periods, such as for work, study, or other purposes, you'll need to explore the available options for temporary residency and work visas. These visas have specific requirements, including proof of financial stability, medical exams, and criminal background checks. It's advisable to consult the Guatemalan consulate or embassy in your home country or a legal expert in Guatemala to understand the application process and documentation required.

Exiting the Country

Upon departure from Guatemala, travelers are often required to pay an exit fee. This fee is typically collected at the airport before your departure flight. Make sure to have enough local currency or U.S. dollars on hand to cover this fee.

COVID-19 Considerations

In light of the ongoing global pandemic, it's crucial to stay updated on any travel restrictions, health protocols, and entry requirements related to COVID-19. As entry regulations and health guidelines can change frequently, it's recommended to check with official government sources, airlines, and local authorities before your trip. This might include requirements for COVID-19 testing, quarantine, or vaccination.

Seeking Professional Advice

Navigating visa and entry requirements can sometimes be complex, depending on your specific circumstances. If you're uncertain about the visa process or your eligibility, consider seeking advice from immigration consultants, legal experts, or the relevant Guatemalan embassy or consulate. These professionals can provide accurate and up-to-date information tailored to your situation.

Understanding the entry requirements and visa information for traveling to Guatemala is an essential step in planning a successful and enjoyable trip. By ensuring that you have the necessary documentation, adhering to immigration regulations, and staying informed about any COVID-19-related guidelines, you can look forward to a seamless experience as you explore the cultural, historical, and natural wonders that Guatemala has to offer.

Health and Safety Tips for Traveling in Guatemala: Navigating a Memorable Journey

As you prepare for an exciting adventure in Guatemala, prioritizing your health and safety is paramount. From exploring ancient ruins to immersing yourself in indigenous cultures and lush landscapes, Guatemala offers a diverse array of experiences. To ensure that your journey is both enjoyable and secure, it's essential to be informed about health precautions, safety considerations, and practical tips that will contribute to a memorable and worry-free trip.

Health Precautions and Vaccinations

Before traveling to Guatemala, it's advisable to consult a travel health professional or visit a travel clinic to discuss recommended vaccinations and health precautions. Common vaccines for travelers include those for hepatitis A and B, typhoid, tetanus, and measles, mumps, and rubella (MMR). Depending on your personal health history and the regions you plan to visit, additional vaccines such as yellow fever and rabies might also be recommended.

Water and Food Safety

Maintaining good hygiene and being cautious about food and water sources is crucial in Guatemala. To avoid waterborne illnesses, it's advisable to drink bottled or boiled water, even when brushing your teeth. When dining, opt for well-cooked and freshly prepared meals. Avoid consuming raw or undercooked meats, salads, and street food unless you are confident about the cleanliness and quality of the vendor.

Insect-Borne Diseases

Guatemala is located in a region where insect-borne diseases such as dengue fever, Zika virus, and chikungunya are a concern. Protect yourself from mosquito bites by wearing long-sleeved clothing, using insect repellent containing DEET, and staying in accommodations with proper mosquito screens and nets. If you develop symptoms such as high fever, severe headache, joint pain, or rash during or after your trip, seek medical attention promptly.

Altitude Sickness

Guatemala's diverse landscapes include highland areas where altitude sickness can be a concern, especially for travelers who are not accustomed to higher elevations. If you plan to visit cities or regions at higher altitudes, such as Antigua or Lake Atitlán, consider acclimatizing gradually and staying hydrated. If you experience symptoms such as shortness of breath, dizziness, or nausea, descend to lower altitudes and seek medical advice if needed.

Medical Facilities and Insurance

While major cities in Guatemala have medical facilities that provide basic medical care, the quality of healthcare can vary. It's recommended to have comprehensive travel insurance that covers medical expenses, including emergency evacuation if necessary. Carry a copy of your insurance policy and emergency contact information with you at all times.

Safety Considerations

Ensuring your safety during your time in Guatemala requires a combination of common sense, awareness, and cultural sensitivity. While Guatemala is generally safe for travelers, it's essential to be cautious and follow these safety tips:

1. Personal Belongings: Keep your belongings secure and be mindful of your surroundings, especially in crowded areas and tourist sites. Use a money belt or hidden pouch to carry your passport, money, and valuables.

2. Transportation: Choose reputable transportation options, especially when traveling long distances or at night. Use registered taxis or transportation services recommended by your accommodation.

3. Street Smarts: Be cautious of petty theft, such as pickpocketing, especially in busy markets and tourist areas. Avoid displaying valuable items and large amounts of cash in public.

4. Local Customs: Respect local customs and traditions, especially when visiting indigenous communities. Always ask for permission before taking photographs of people, and dress modestly when required by cultural norms.

5. Demonstrations and Protests: Avoid participating in or being near political demonstrations or protests, as these events can sometimes become unpredictable.

6. Adventure Activities: If you're planning to participate in adventure activities such as hiking or volcano climbing, choose licensed operators that prioritize safety and adhere to proper equipment standards.

Emergency Contacts

Before embarking on your journey, save important phone numbers in your phone and jot them down in a travel journal:

- Tourist Police: 1500

- Medical Emergencies: 911

- U.S. Embassy in Guatemala City: +502 2326-4000

- Your Country's Embassy or Consulate

Cultural Sensitivity and Etiquette

Respecting the local culture and customs enhances both your safety and the quality of your experience. Dress modestly when visiting religious sites or indigenous communities, and ask for permission before taking photographs. Learning a few basic phrases in Spanish, such as greetings and expressions of gratitude, can go a long way in establishing positive interactions with locals.

By prioritizing your health and safety during your trip to Guatemala, you're not only ensuring a more enjoyable experience but also contributing to a positive interaction with the country and

its people. Armed with knowledge about health precautions, safety considerations, and local customs, you can embark on your journey with confidence, curiosity, and a sense of adventure, ready to embrace the wonders that Guatemala has to offer.

The Importance of Travel Insurance: Protecting Your Journey to Guatemala

As you plan your upcoming adventure to Guatemala, there's an essential aspect that should be at the top of your checklist: travel insurance. While exploring ancient ruins, immersing yourself in vibrant cultures, and venturing through lush landscapes, unexpected events can disrupt even the most meticulously planned trips. Travel insurance provides a safety net that safeguards your investment, health, and well-being, allowing you to explore Guatemala with peace of mind. This comprehensive guide will delve into the various aspects of travel insurance, from understanding its benefits to choosing the right policy for your journey.

Understanding Travel Insurance

Travel insurance is a type of insurance that offers coverage and protection against unexpected events that may occur before or during your trip. These events can range from trip cancellations and delays to medical emergencies, lost baggage, and more. Travel insurance provides financial assistance and support in navigating challenging situations that might otherwise lead to financial losses or disruptions.

Benefits of Travel Insurance

1. Trip Cancellation or Interruption: Life is unpredictable, and sometimes plans change. Travel insurance can reimburse you for non-refundable trip costs if you need to cancel or cut short your trip due to covered reasons such as illness, injury, or unforeseen events.

2. Medical Emergencies: Medical expenses can be exorbitant, especially if you require medical attention in a foreign country. Travel insurance covers medical treatment, hospital stays, and emergency medical evacuations, ensuring you receive necessary care without incurring significant financial burdens.

3. Travel Delays: Flight cancellations, missed connections, and weather-related delays are common travel frustrations. Travel insurance can provide reimbursement for additional accommodation, meals, and transportation expenses incurred due to unexpected delays.

4. Lost or Delayed Baggage: If your luggage is lost, damaged, or delayed by the airline, travel insurance can cover the cost of replacing essential items, such as clothing and toiletries, while you're away from home.

5. Emergency Assistance: When you're in an unfamiliar environment, having access to a 24/7 emergency assistance hotline can be invaluable. Travel insurance can help you navigate medical referrals, translation services, and other emergencies.

6. Personal Liability: Accidents happen, and travel insurance can offer coverage for personal liability in case you're involved in an incident that causes injury or property damage to others.

Choosing the Right Policy

With various travel insurance providers and policies available, selecting the right one for your needs requires careful consideration. Here are some factors to keep in mind:

1. Coverage Limits: Review the coverage limits for medical expenses, trip cancellation, baggage loss, and other benefits. Make sure the limits align with your travel plans and potential expenses.

2. Pre-Existing Conditions: Some policies offer coverage for pre-existing medical conditions, while others may not. If you have a pre-existing condition, ensure that the policy covers it.

3. Activities and Adventure: If you plan to engage in adventure activities such as hiking, zip-lining, or volcano climbing, confirm that the policy provides coverage for these activities.

4. Deductibles: Consider the deductible amount you're comfortable with. A higher deductible might result in a lower premium but could also require you to pay more out of pocket in the event of a claim.

5. Exclusions: Read the policy exclusions carefully to understand what is not covered. Common exclusions may include alcohol-related incidents, illegal activities, and extreme sports.

6. Cancel for Any Reason (CFAR) Coverage: Some policies offer CFAR coverage, which allows you to cancel your trip for any reason and receive a partial refund. This can provide additional flexibility, but it often comes at a higher cost.

7. Length of Coverage: Ensure that the coverage period aligns with the duration of your trip. If you plan to extend your stay, inquire about the possibility of extending your coverage as well.

8. Group and Family Plans: If you're traveling with a group or family, inquire about group or family coverage options, which can sometimes be more cost-effective.

9. Review Policy Details: Before purchasing travel insurance, carefully review the policy documents, terms, and conditions. Pay attention to the fine print to understand the specifics of coverage, claims procedures, and contact information.

When to Purchase Travel Insurance

Ideally, you should purchase travel insurance as soon as you've made non-refundable payments toward your trip. This ensures that you're covered for unexpected events that might arise before your departure. Waiting until the last minute to buy travel insurance might limit your coverage options.

Claim Process and Documentation

In the event of a covered incident, it's crucial to follow the proper claim process outlined in your policy. This might involve contacting the insurance provider's claims department, providing

documentation of the incident, and completing claim forms. Documenting incidents with photographs, receipts, and medical reports can expedite the claims process.

Investing in travel insurance is a smart and responsible decision that provides a safety net for your journey to Guatemala. From medical emergencies to unexpected cancellations, travel insurance offers peace of mind, allowing you to focus on exploring, experiencing, and creating unforgettable memories. By carefully selecting the right policy and understanding the coverage it provides, you're ensuring that your trip to Guatemala is not only enjoyable but also secure and worry-free.

Packing Essentials for Your Journey to Guatemala: Navigating a Dynamic Adventure

Packing for a trip to Guatemala requires careful consideration of the country's diverse landscapes, varying climates, cultural experiences, and outdoor adventures. Whether you're exploring ancient ruins, relaxing by serene lakes, or immersing yourself in indigenous cultures, having the right packing essentials can greatly enhance your travel experience. This comprehensive guide will help you create a well-rounded packing list that ensures you're prepared for the journey ahead.

Clothing and Footwear

1. Lightweight Clothing: Guatemala's climate can vary from region to region, so pack a mix of lightweight, breathable clothing suitable for both warm and cooler weather. Opt for clothing that can be layered for temperature fluctuations.

2. Long-Sleeved Shirts and Pants: Long-sleeved shirts and pants can protect you from the sun, insects, and cooler evenings. Lightweight, quick-drying fabrics are ideal.

3. Rain Jacket or Poncho: Given Guatemala's varying weather patterns, a compact rain jacket or poncho is a valuable addition to your packing list.

4. Swimsuit: Don't forget your swimsuit, especially if you plan to relax by Lake Atitlán or explore the coastal areas.

5. Comfortable Footwear: Bring comfortable walking shoes or hiking boots for exploring archaeological sites and hiking trails. A pair of sandals or flip-flops is also handy for casual outings.

6. Hat and Sunglasses: Protect yourself from the sun with a wide-brimmed hat and quality sunglasses.

7. Warm Layer: If you're planning to visit highland areas, such as Antigua, consider packing a warm layer for cooler evenings.

Essential Accessories

1. Daypack or Backpack: A lightweight, sturdy daypack is essential for carrying water, snacks, a camera, and other essentials during your daily adventures.

2. Reusable Water Bottle: Stay hydrated by carrying a reusable water bottle that you can refill throughout the day.

3. Money Belt or Hidden Pouch:*I Keep your passport, money, and important documents secure with a discreet money belt or hidden pouch.

4. Travel Adapter and Power Bank: Guatemala uses Type A and Type B electrical outlets. Don't forget a travel adapter and power bank to keep your devices charged.

5. Basic First Aid Kit: Pack essentials such as adhesive bandages, pain relievers, antiseptic wipes, and any personal medications you may need.

Personal Care and Toiletries

1. Sunscreen: Protect your skin from the strong Central American sun with a high SPF sunscreen.

2. Insect Repellent: A good-quality insect repellent is crucial for protecting yourself against mosquito-borne illnesses.

3. Hand Sanitizer: Keep a small bottle of hand sanitizer with you for situations where soap and water aren't readily available.

4. Toiletries: Pack travel-sized toiletries, including toothpaste, toothbrush, shampoo, and any other personal care items you require.

Electronics and Gadgets

1. Camera: Capture the beauty of Guatemala with a camera or smartphone with a good camera function.

2. Phone and Charger: Bring your phone for communication and navigation. Consider downloading offline maps for areas with limited connectivity.

3. Headlamp or Flashlight: A headlamp or small flashlight can be useful, especially if you're exploring areas with limited lighting.

Documents and Essentials

1. Passport: Ensure your passport is valid for at least six months beyond your planned return date.

2. Visa and Entry Documents: If required, carry a printout of your visa or entry documents.

3. Travel Insurance: Carry a copy of your travel insurance policy and emergency contact information.

4. Prescriptions: If you have any prescriptions, bring enough medication for the duration of your trip.

5. Cash and Credit Cards: While credit cards are widely accepted, it's advisable to carry some local currency for smaller establishments.

6. Photocopies and Digital Copies: Make photocopies of important documents, such as your passport and travel insurance, and store digital copies securely.

Cultural Sensitivity

When packing clothing for your trip, consider the cultural norms of Guatemala. Modesty is appreciated, especially when visiting religious sites and indigenous communities. Pack clothing that covers your shoulders and knees to show respect for local traditions.

Pack Light and Pack Right

Efficient packing involves striking a balance between having what you need and avoiding overpacking. Keep in mind that you can purchase certain items locally if necessary, such as toiletries and clothing. Opt for versatile clothing pieces that can be mixed and matched, and focus on quality rather than quantity.

Packing for a trip to Guatemala is an exciting part of the travel process. By packing smartly and considering the diverse experiences you'll encounter, you can ensure that you have everything you need for a comfortable and enriching journey. From the essentials that keep you safe and prepared to the items that enhance your cultural immersion, a well-curated packing list sets the stage for a memorable adventure filled with exploration, discovery, and unforgettable moments.

Section 3: Getting to Guatemala

Airports and International Connections

Guatemala is well-connected internationally through several airports, with La Aurora International Airport (GUA) in Guatemala City being the primary gateway. Here are some of the best airports and international connections in Guatemala:

1. La Aurora International Airport (GUA) – Guatemala City:

- La Aurora International Airport is the main international gateway to Guatemala. It's located in the capital city, Guatemala City, and serves as the hub for both domestic and international flights.

- The airport offers a wide range of international connections to destinations in North America, Central America, South America, Europe, and beyond.

- Major airlines such as American Airlines, Delta Air Lines, United Airlines, Avianca, Copa Airlines, and more operate flights to and from La Aurora International Airport.

2. Mundo Maya International Airport (FRS) – Flores:

- Mundo Maya International Airport is located near the town of Flores in the Petén department of northern Guatemala.

- It primarily serves travelers heading to the nearby UNESCO-listed ancient Mayan ruins of Tikal, one of the most significant archaeological sites in the region.

- The airport has connections to Guatemala City as well as some international charter flights.

3. Ramón Villeda Morales International Airport (SAP) – San Pedro Sula, Honduras:

- While not located in Guatemala, Ramón Villeda Morales International Airport in San Pedro Sula, Honduras, is an important hub for travelers coming to and from western Guatemala.

- It serves as a gateway for travelers heading to destinations like Copán Ruinas and the western highlands of Guatemala.

4. Juan José Arévalo Bermejo Airport (GUA) – Puerto Barrios:

- Located in Puerto Barrios on the Caribbean coast of Guatemala, this airport provides an alternative entry point for travelers arriving by air.

- It's mainly used for domestic flights and serves as a gateway to the eastern and Caribbean areas of Guatemala.

5. Quetzaltenango Airport (AAQ) – Quetzaltenango (Xela):

- Quetzaltenango Airport, also known as Los Altos Airport, is located in the city of Quetzaltenango, often referred to as Xela.

- While primarily used for domestic flights, it can be useful for travelers exploring the western highlands.

6. San José Airport (GSJ) – San José, Petén:

- San José Airport is located in San José, a town near the popular tourist destination of Tikal.

- It's a smaller airport that serves mainly domestic flights and provides access to Tikal and other nearby attractions.

Connecting from Major International Hubs:

- Many travelers connect to Guatemala through major international airports in nearby countries, such as Mexico City International Airport, Houston's George Bush Intercontinental Airport, Miami International Airport, and Panama City's Tocumen International Airport.

- These major hubs offer a wide range of flights to La Aurora International Airport in Guatemala City.

Guatemala offers several airports for international connections, with La Aurora International Airport in Guatemala City being the primary gateway. Whether you're exploring the Mayan ruins, highland towns, or vibrant markets, these airports provide convenient access to the diverse experiences that Guatemala has to offer.

La Aurora International Airport (GUA) – Guatemala City: A Gateway to Guatemala's Rich Culture and Natural Beauty

La Aurora International Airport (GUA) serves as the main gateway to Guatemala, connecting travelers from around the world to the heart of Central America's diverse landscapes, rich culture, and historical heritage. Located in the capital city of Guatemala, Guatemala City, the airport is a bustling hub that welcomes visitors with modern facilities, convenient services, and a glimpse into the warmth and hospitality that define Guatemalan culture. In this comprehensive guide, we'll explore the features, services, and experiences that make La Aurora International Airport an essential part of any traveler's journey to Guatemala.

La Aurora International Airport is conveniently situated within the city limits of Guatemala City, the country's capital. Its central location makes it easily accessible from various parts of the city, ensuring a seamless transition from the airport to your chosen destination.

The airport comprises a main terminal building with multiple levels and sections that cater to the needs of both domestic and international travelers. The terminal is equipped with modern amenities, including lounges, shops, restaurants, and services that enhance the overall travel experience.

Upon arrival, passengers are guided through the immigration process, where passports and entry documents are checked. The efficient immigration procedures ensure that travelers can swiftly move through the arrival process and begin their Guatemalan adventure without unnecessary delays.

La Aurora International Airport boasts a well-organized baggage claim area where travelers can collect their checked luggage. After retrieving their baggage, passengers proceed through customs clearance, where any required declarations are made and customs regulations are adhered to.

The airport offers a range of transportation options to help travelers reach their final destinations. These include taxis, shuttle services, and car rental agencies. Whether you're heading to the vibrant markets of Antigua, the ancient ruins of Tikal, or the picturesque shores of Lake Atitlán, there are convenient transportation solutions to suit your needs.

The airport's duty-free shopping area provides an opportunity for travelers to purchase a variety of goods, from local handicrafts to international luxury brands. This is an ideal place to pick up unique souvenirs that reflect Guatemala's vibrant culture and heritage.

La Aurora International Airport offers a diverse array of dining options to cater to different tastes and preferences. From traditional Guatemalan cuisine to international fare, passengers can enjoy a meal or snack that suits their cravings before or after their flights.

For travelers seeking an elevated level of comfort and relaxation, the airport features VIP lounges where guests can unwind, catch up on work, or enjoy refreshments while waiting for their flights.

The airport provides currency exchange services to facilitate smooth transactions for international travelers. Additionally, there are banking facilities and ATMs available for accessing cash and conducting financial transactions.

Travelers' well-being is a priority at La Aurora International Airport. The airport is equipped with medical facilities and trained staff to assist passengers in case of medical emergencies.

Staying connected while traveling is made easy at the airport, thanks to Wi-Fi services that allow passengers to access the internet and stay in touch with loved ones.

La Aurora International Airport showcases elements of Guatemalan culture through art installations, exhibits, and architectural designs. The airport provides a glimpse into the country's history, traditions, and artistic expressions, allowing travelers to begin immersing themselves in the local culture from the moment they arrive.

In recent years, the airport has taken steps to implement environmentally friendly practices, including waste management, energy conservation, and sustainability efforts. These initiatives reflect a commitment to minimizing the airport's impact on the environment and contributing to a greener future.

La Aurora International Airport serves as an inviting entry point to the captivating world of Guatemala. Beyond its role as a transportation hub, the airport offers a preview of the country's warm hospitality, rich culture, and diverse landscapes. From modern facilities to convenient services, La Aurora International Airport ensures that travelers embark on their Guatemalan journey with ease, comfort, and a sense of excitement for the experiences that await them. Whether you're arriving to explore ancient Mayan ruins, soak in natural hot springs, or immerse yourself in indigenous traditions, the airport's welcoming atmosphere sets the tone for a memorable and enriching adventure in the heart of Central America.

Mundo Maya International Airport (FRS) – Flores: Your Gateway to Guatemala's Ancient Mayan Treasures

Mundo Maya International Airport (FRS) serves as a vital gateway for travelers eager to explore the ancient wonders of the Mayan civilization in the Petén region of Guatemala. Nestled near the charming town of Flores, this airport provides easy access to the UNESCO-listed archaeological site of Tikal and other captivating destinations in the northern part of the country. In this comprehensive guide, we will delve into the features, services, and experiences that make Mundo Maya International Airport a pivotal point of entry for those seeking to unravel the mysteries of Guatemala's past.

Mundo Maya International Airport is strategically located near the town of Flores, which sits on an island on Lake Petén Itzá. This proximity to Flores ensures that travelers are just a short distance away from their chosen accommodations, allowing them to quickly embark on their exploration of the ancient Mayan ruins.

The airport features a single terminal with facilities designed to cater to both domestic and international travelers. Despite its relatively modest size, the terminal is equipped with modern amenities that contribute to a seamless and enjoyable travel experience.

Travelers arriving at Mundo Maya International Airport undergo immigration procedures, which include passport and document checks. The efficiency of these processes ensures that visitors can promptly transition from their flights to the exciting adventures that await them in the Petén region.

The airport's well-organized baggage claim area enables passengers to swiftly retrieve their checked luggage upon arrival. Afterward, travelers proceed through customs clearance, adhering to regulations and declarations as required.

Upon exiting the airport, travelers have various transportation options available to take them to their intended destinations. Taxis, shuttle services, and rental cars are readily accessible, allowing visitors to efficiently reach their accommodations and embark on their exploration of the area.

Mundo Maya International Airport embraces Guatemala's rich cultural heritage through art installations, exhibits, and architectural designs. Passengers are greeted with elements that pay homage to the ancient Mayan civilization, setting the tone for their upcoming adventures to historical sites.

One of the most significant advantages of Mundo Maya International Airport is its proximity to Tikal, one of the largest and most well-preserved Mayan archaeological sites in the world. Travelers who step off their flights at this airport are just a short distance away from exploring Tikal's towering pyramids, intricate temples, and ancient plazas that offer a glimpse into the Mayan civilization's architectural and cultural achievements.

In addition to Tikal, Mundo Maya International Airport provides access to Lake Petén Itzá and its surrounding areas. The charming town of Flores, with its cobblestone streets and colorful buildings, is a popular destination for travelers. The lake itself offers opportunities for water-based activities, such as kayaking, swimming, and boat tours.

While Tikal is the crown jewel of the region, Mundo Maya International Airport also opens the door to other archaeological sites and lesser-known Mayan ruins. Visitors can venture beyond Tikal to explore Yaxhá, El Mirador, and other sites that contribute to a comprehensive understanding of the Mayan civilization's history and legacy.

Beyond the historical sites, the Petén region is known for its impressive biodiversity and natural beauty. Travelers can take advantage of Mundo Maya International Airport's proximity to national parks and reserves, such as the Maya Biosphere Reserve, which encompasses both historical sites and thriving ecosystems.

Mundo Maya International Airport serves as the starting point for travelers seeking not only to explore archaeological sites but also to immerse themselves in the modern-day indigenous cultures of the region. Interactions with local communities, visits to traditional markets, and participation in cultural events contribute to a well-rounded travel experience.

Mundo Maya International Airport is more than just an airport; it's a gateway to the heart of Guatemala's ancient Mayan treasures. As travelers step off their flights and onto Guatemalan soil, they embark on a journey that bridges the past and the present, offering a window into the country's rich history, vibrant culture, and awe-inspiring natural landscapes. Whether you're exploring the towering pyramids of Tikal, connecting with local communities, or discovering the diverse ecosystems of the Petén region, Mundo Maya International Airport sets the stage for an adventure that promises to be as enlightening as it is enchanting.

Ramón Villeda Morales International Airport (SAP) – Connecting Guatemala and Beyond from San Pedro Sula, Honduras

Ramón Villeda Morales International Airport (SAP) serves as a significant transportation hub connecting travelers to and from western Guatemala and beyond. Located in San Pedro Sula, Honduras, this airport offers a vital gateway for those seeking to explore the diverse landscapes, cultural richness, and historical wonders of both Honduras and neighboring Guatemala. In this comprehensive guide, we will delve into the features, services, and experiences that make Ramón Villeda Morales International Airport an important point of entry for those embarking on their Central American adventures.

Ramón Villeda Morales International Airport is situated in the city of San Pedro Sula, the economic and industrial center of Honduras. Its central location in the region makes it an easily accessible option for travelers from both Honduras and neighboring countries.

The airport features a modern terminal equipped to handle both domestic and international flights. Travelers are welcomed with facilities designed to enhance their comfort and convenience throughout their journey.

Upon arrival at Ramón Villeda Morales International Airport, passengers proceed through immigration procedures, where passports and entry documents are reviewed. The airport's efficient processes ensure that travelers can quickly transition from their flights to their next destination.

The airport provides a well-organized baggage claim area, allowing travelers to promptly retrieve their checked luggage. Following baggage claim, passengers proceed through customs clearance, adhering to required regulations and declarations.

Ramón Villeda Morales International Airport offers a range of transportation options for passengers to reach their desired destinations. These options include taxis, shuttle services, and car rental agencies, ensuring that travelers can conveniently continue their journeys.

The airport facilitates communication and connectivity for travelers through Wi-Fi services, allowing passengers to stay connected with loved ones and access essential information during their time at the airport.

While Ramón Villeda Morales International Airport is located in Honduras, it plays a role in connecting travelers to the cultural tapestry of both Honduras and neighboring Guatemala.

Travelers arriving at this airport are embarking on a journey that promises to showcase the diverse cultural heritage of the Central American region.

One of the significant advantages of Ramón Villeda Morales International Airport is its role as a connecting point for travelers heading to western Guatemala. This airport provides a convenient route for those interested in exploring destinations such as Copán Ruinas, a UNESCO World Heritage Site known for its ancient Mayan ruins and archaeological significance.

Ramón Villeda Morales International Airport's proximity to Copán Ruinas makes it an ideal entry point for travelers seeking to immerse themselves in the history and architecture of the ancient Mayan civilization. Copán Ruins, with its intricate stelae, hieroglyphic staircases, and ceremonial plazas, offers a captivating glimpse into the achievements and culture of the Mayan people.

Beyond its cultural and historical attractions, the western regions of both Honduras and Guatemala are known for their natural beauty. Ramón Villeda Morales International Airport provides travelers with access to lush landscapes, national parks, and opportunities for eco-tourism and outdoor adventures.

Ramón Villeda Morales International Airport serves as a gateway for travelers interested in exploring the highland areas of western Guatemala. This region includes destinations such as Quetzaltenango (Xela), known for its indigenous culture, colonial architecture, and proximity to the towering Santa María volcano.

Ramón Villeda Morales International Airport is more than just an airport; it's a bridge connecting travelers to the rich cultural heritage, historical wonders, and natural beauty of both Honduras and western Guatemala. As passengers step off their flights and onto Central American soil, they are embarking on an adventure that promises to be both enlightening and immersive. Whether you're exploring ancient Mayan ruins, discovering indigenous traditions, or marveling at the diverse landscapes, the airport serves as the starting point for a journey that captures the essence of this vibrant and captivating region.

Quetzaltenango Airport (AAQ) – Quetzaltenango (Xela): Unveiling the Gateway to Guatemala's Highland Heart

Quetzaltenango Airport (AAQ), located in the city of Quetzaltenango, often referred to as Xela, stands as a key entry point to the breathtaking highland landscapes and rich cultural tapestry of Guatemala. Nestled amidst the western highlands, this airport offers travelers an opportunity to immerse themselves in the indigenous traditions, colonial charm, and volcanic vistas that define

this region. In this comprehensive guide, we will delve into the features, services, and experiences that make Quetzaltenango Airport a gateway to the enchanting world of Guatemala's highland heart.

Quetzaltenango Airport is situated in the city of Quetzaltenango, the second-largest city in Guatemala and a vibrant hub of culture, history, and education. Its strategic location in the western highlands provides travelers with access to a region renowned for its natural beauty and cultural significance.

The airport's terminal is designed to accommodate both domestic and international travelers, providing essential amenities and services that enhance the overall travel experience.

Upon arrival, passengers at Quetzaltenango Airport go through immigration procedures, where passports and entry documents are reviewed. The efficient immigration processes ensure that travelers can swiftly move from their flights to the captivating experiences that await them.

The airport's well-organized baggage claim area allows passengers to promptly retrieve their checked luggage upon arrival. After collecting their baggage, travelers proceed through customs clearance, adhering to regulations and declarations as required.

Upon leaving the airport, travelers have various transportation options available to take them to their desired destinations. Taxis, shuttle services, and local transportation provide convenient choices to continue their journey in the highlands.

Quetzaltenango, often referred to as Xela (pronounced "shay-la"), welcomes visitors with a unique blend of indigenous culture, colonial architecture, and educational institutions. The city's historic center is adorned with colorful buildings, charming squares, and bustling markets.

Quetzaltenango Airport serves as a pivotal entry point for travelers interested in exploring the picturesque western highlands of Guatemala. This region encompasses towering volcanoes, indigenous villages, and a tapestry of cultural experiences that capture the essence of Guatemalan highland life.

Travelers arriving at Quetzaltenango Airport have the opportunity to connect with the indigenous communities that call the highlands home. The nearby village of San Andrés Xecul is known for its vibrant yellow church, a symbol of the blend of Mayan spirituality and Catholicism.

The western highlands are dominated by a series of dramatic volcanoes, and Quetzaltenango Airport serves as a gateway to the adventure of climbing these peaks. Volcanoes such as Santa María and Santiaguito offer exhilarating hikes and the chance to witness live volcanic activity.

Xela is renowned for its language schools, making it a popular destination for travelers interested in learning Spanish while immersing themselves in the local culture. Quetzaltenango Airport introduces visitors to an educational atmosphere that extends beyond the classroom.

The region around Quetzaltenango is known for its thermal baths and natural hot springs. After an adventurous day of exploring, travelers can unwind and rejuvenate in the therapeutic waters while gazing at the surrounding landscapes.

Traveling to Quetzaltenango Airport and the surrounding region contributes to the economic development of local communities. From purchasing traditional handicrafts to engaging with local guides and businesses, visitors have the opportunity to make a positive impact.

Quetzaltenango Airport (AAQ) serves as a gateway to the captivating landscapes, indigenous cultures, and enriching experiences of Guatemala's western highlands. As travelers disembark from their flights and set foot in the city of Xela, they step into a world where tradition meets modernity, where colonial charm harmonizes with volcanoes' grandeur, and where the heart of Guatemala's cultural tapestry beats strong. Whether you're exploring indigenous markets, climbing volcanoes, or embracing the city's educational atmosphere, the airport is the starting point for an adventure that captures the essence of this enchanting highland region.

San José Airport (GSJ) – San José, Petén: Your Portal to Exploring the Ancient Mayan Wonders

San José Airport (GSJ) serves as a unique entry point to the captivating world of ancient Mayan wonders in the Petén region of Guatemala. Nestled near the historical treasure trove of Tikal and the charming town of Flores, this airport offers travelers an opportunity to step back in time and immerse themselves in the mysteries of the Mayan civilization. In this comprehensive guide, we will delve into the features, services, and experiences that make San José Airport a portal to the enchanting history and natural beauty that define the heart of Guatemala.

San José Airport is conveniently located near the town of San José, a gateway to the Petén region's historical and natural attractions. Its proximity to Tikal and Flores ensures that travelers can quickly access their desired destinations upon arrival.

The airport's terminal is designed to accommodate both domestic and international travelers, providing essential amenities and services that contribute to a seamless travel experience.

Upon arrival, passengers proceed through immigration procedures, where passports and entry documents are reviewed. The efficient immigration processes ensure that travelers can swiftly move from their flights to the captivating experiences that await them.

The airport's organized baggage claim area allows passengers to promptly retrieve their checked luggage upon arrival. After collecting their baggage, travelers proceed through customs clearance, adhering to regulations and declarations as required.

Upon exiting the airport, travelers have various transportation options available to take them to their intended destinations. Taxis, shuttle services, and local transportation provide convenient choices to continue their journey in the Petén region.

San José Airport stands as a pivotal entry point for travelers eager to explore the marvels of Tikal, one of the most iconic Mayan archaeological sites in the world. As travelers disembark from their flights, they are poised to embark on a journey through time, uncovering the mysteries of an ancient civilization.

The airport serves as a gateway to Tikal's towering pyramids, sprawling plazas, and intricate temples that showcase the architectural brilliance of the Mayan people. Travelers can walk in the footsteps of the ancients, marveling at the grandeur of a civilization that once thrived in these lush jungles.

Beyond the historical sites, the Petén region boasts remarkable natural beauty and biodiversity. San José Airport offers access to the sprawling Maya Biosphere Reserve, where travelers can witness the coexistence of archaeological treasures and flourishing ecosystems.

One of the highlights of visiting Tikal is the opportunity to witness a breathtaking sunrise over the ancient ruins. Travelers who arrive at San José Airport have the chance to embark on this unforgettable experience, watching as the jungle awakens to reveal the splendor of Tikal.

The region surrounding Tikal is a haven for wildlife enthusiasts and birdwatchers. Toucans, howler monkeys, and a diverse array of species call this area home, offering travelers the chance to observe Guatemala's vibrant biodiversity up close.

While Tikal is the crown jewel of the region, San José Airport also facilitates interactions with the modern-day descendants of the Mayan civilization. Travelers can connect with indigenous communities, learn about their traditions, and gain insights into their way of life.

San José Airport also offers access to the charming town of Flores, located on an island on Lake Petén Itzá. Flores is a picturesque destination with cobblestone streets, colorful buildings, and a laid-back atmosphere.

Visiting Tikal and the surrounding areas contributes to the preservation of these historical treasures. Fees collected from entry tickets support conservation efforts, ensuring that future generations can continue to marvel at the wonders of the past.

San José Airport (GSJ) serves as a doorway to the captivating history, natural beauty, and cultural richness of the Petén region in Guatemala. As travelers step off their flights and onto the soil of this remarkable region, they enter a world where ancient wonders come to life, where lush jungles conceal architectural marvels, and where the echoes of the Mayan civilization resonate through time. Whether you're exploring the towering pyramids of Tikal, witnessing a sunrise over ancient temples, or connecting with indigenous communities, the airport serves as the starting point for an adventure that captures the essence of Guatemala's historical and natural treasures.

Land Border Crossings

Guatemala offers several land border crossings that allow travelers to enter or exit the country. These border crossings are important gateways for those exploring neighboring countries, experiencing cross-cultural interactions, and embarking on overland journeys. Here are some of the best land border crossings in Guatemala:

1. La Mesilla – Mexico:

This border crossing connects Guatemala with Mexico's southern state of Chiapas. It's a popular route for travelers moving between the two countries. La Mesilla is near the city of Huehuetenango in Guatemala and connects to the Mexican town of Ciudad Cuauhtémoc. The crossing is well-traveled and provides easy access to destinations like San Cristóbal de las Casas and Palenque in Mexico.

2. El Florido – Mexico:

Situated in the western part of Guatemala near the town of Malacatán, El Florido is another key border crossing with Mexico. It connects to the Mexican city of Tecún Umán in the state of Chiapas. This crossing is often used by travelers heading to or from the Mexican Pacific coast and destinations like Tapachula.

3. Agua Caliente – Honduras:

Connecting Guatemala with western Honduras, the Agua Caliente border crossing is an important gateway for travelers moving between these two countries. On the Guatemalan side, the border is near Esquipulas, which is known for its basilica and religious pilgrimages. On the Honduran side, the border is near Copán Ruinas, a UNESCO-listed archaeological site.

4. La Palma – El Salvador:

Located in the western part of Guatemala, the La Palma border crossing connects with El Salvador. It's near the Guatemalan town of Jutiapa and connects to the Salvadoran town of La Palma. This crossing is convenient for those traveling between western Guatemala and destinations in El Salvador, such as Santa Ana or San Salvador.

5. Valle Nuevo – El Salvador:

Another border crossing between Guatemala and El Salvador, Valle Nuevo, connects the Guatemalan town of Atescatempa with the Salvadoran town of Jocotán. This crossing is useful for travelers exploring the eastern parts of both countries.

6. Gracias a Dios – Belize:

For those looking to cross into Belize, the Gracias a Dios border crossing is a key entry point. It connects the Guatemalan town of Melchor de Mencos with the Belizean town of Benque Viejo del Carmen. This crossing is often used by travelers exploring the diverse attractions of Belize, such as its pristine beaches and vibrant marine life.

7. Santa Elena – Belize:

Near the famous Mayan ruins of Tikal, the Santa Elena border crossing connects the Guatemalan town of Flores with the Belizean town of San Ignacio. This crossing is particularly convenient for travelers combining visits to Tikal and Belize's Cayo District.

8. San Cristóbal – Mexico:

Situated in the southern part of Guatemala, the San Cristóbal border crossing connects with the Mexican town of Comitán de Domínguez in Chiapas. While not as busy as some other crossings, it's used by travelers exploring the southern regions of Guatemala and Mexico.

When crossing any border, it's essential to have all necessary travel documents, including passports, visas, and any required permits. Border crossing regulations can change, so it's recommended to check with relevant authorities or official sources before embarking on your journey.

La Mesilla – Mexico: A Crossroads of Culture and Connectivity

The border crossing of La Mesilla, connecting Guatemala and Mexico, is more than just a geographical intersection—it's a portal that bridges cultures, histories, and experiences. Situated in the western highlands of Guatemala, near the town of Huehuetenango, La Mesilla serves as a vibrant gateway to Mexico's southern state of Chiapas. As travelers cross this border, they embark on a journey that transcends national boundaries and offers a glimpse into the shared heritage and diverse landscapes of Central America and Mexico.

La Mesilla border crossing holds a strategic position in the western part of Guatemala. It's situated in close proximity to Huehuetenango, a city that stands as a crossroads of indigenous cultures, trade routes, and historical significance. The border's location allows travelers to seamlessly transition between two distinct countries while exploring the captivating landscapes that define this region.

At the heart of La Mesilla's significance is its role as a cultural intersection. As travelers cross the border, they encounter a fusion of Mayan heritage, indigenous traditions, and Mexican culture. This convergence creates a rich tapestry of experiences that resonate with both historical depth and contemporary vibrancy.

The surrounding region is home to diverse Mayan communities, each with its own language, customs, and traditions. The border crossing is a testament to the enduring legacy of indigenous peoples in this part of the world. As travelers interact with local residents, they gain insights into the daily lives, artistic expressions, and spiritual beliefs that shape the identity of these communities.

La Mesilla has long been a hub of commercial activity, serving as a meeting point for traders, merchants, and travelers. This tradition continues today, as bustling markets showcase an array of goods, from textiles to handicrafts. The border's proximity to both Huehuetenango and Mexico's Chiapas region contributes to the exchange of products, ideas, and cultural influences.

The history of La Mesilla is interwoven with tales of colonization, struggle, and resilience. The border area witnessed historical events that shaped the destinies of both Guatemala and Mexico. Understanding the past is essential to comprehending the context in which these cultures have evolved and continue to interact.

As travelers cross the border, they step into the Mexican state of Chiapas—an enchanting region characterized by lush landscapes, vibrant markets, and diverse communities. The proximity to Chiapas grants visitors access to an array of experiences, from exploring the colonial charm of San Cristóbal de las Casas to delving into the natural wonders of the Sumidero Canyon.

The journey across La Mesilla is marked by cultural discoveries that extend beyond national borders. From savoring traditional Guatemalan cuisine to indulging in Mexican street food, travelers are treated to a sensory feast that exemplifies the fusion of flavors, aromas, and culinary traditions.

The landscapes surrounding La Mesilla and its Mexican counterpart are characterized by their natural beauty and biodiversity. From the rugged highlands of Guatemala to the rainforests and coffee plantations of Chiapas, this region is a haven for nature enthusiasts and adventure seekers alike.

La Mesilla border crossing is a site of connection, where interactions between travelers, locals, and fellow explorers shape shared experiences. The friendships forged and stories exchanged at this crossroads contribute to the mutual understanding and cultural exchange that define modern-day travel.

As La Mesilla becomes more accessible to travelers, a responsibility arises to approach this cultural intersection with respect and mindfulness. Embracing sustainable tourism practices helps ensure that the authenticity of the region's cultures, traditions, and environments remains intact for generations to come.

La Mesilla border crossing is more than a point on a map; it's a passage that transcends boundaries and invites travelers to embark on a journey of exploration, discovery, and connection. As individuals cross this threshold, they enter a realm where cultures intertwine, histories unfold, and shared experiences are woven into the fabric of the human story. Whether it's the vibrant markets, the indigenous communities, or the natural landscapes, La Mesilla beckons travelers to venture beyond borders and embrace the beauty of cross-cultural encounters.

El Florido – Mexico: Crossing Borders and Embracing Diversity

The El Florido border crossing stands as a dynamic crossroads that connects Guatemala and Mexico, facilitating the flow of people, goods, and cultures between these two vibrant nations. Located in the western reaches of Guatemala near the town of Malacatán, El Florido is a gateway to the southern Mexican state of Chiapas. This border crossing is more than a mere geographical intersection—it's a testament to the shared histories, cultural exchange, and human connections that define the relationship between Central America and Mexico.

El Florido holds a strategic position in the western highlands of Guatemala, a region characterized by its rugged landscapes and indigenous heritage. This border crossing provides a vital link between Malacatán and Ciudad Hidalgo, a Mexican town in Chiapas. The geographical significance of El Florido extends beyond its coordinates; it embodies the spirit of unity that transcends national borders.

At the heart of El Florido's significance is its role as a conduit for cultural exchange. As travelers cross the border, they move between two countries that share historical ties, linguistic diversity, and a tapestry of traditions. The interplay of Guatemalan Mayan culture and Mexican influences creates a mosaic of experiences that enrich the journey across this crossroads.

The surrounding region is steeped in Mayan heritage, with indigenous communities that have preserved their languages, customs, and ancestral knowledge. The border crossing serves as a reminder of the enduring legacy of the Mayan civilization, as it connects modern travelers with the traditions and beliefs that have shaped this part of the world for centuries.

El Florido has a history as a hub of trade and interaction. This tradition continues to flourish, as markets and cross-border commerce highlight the economic interdependence between the two countries. The proximity of Malacatán to Ciudad Hidalgo contributes to the exchange of products, ideas, and cultural experiences that define the dynamic border region.

El Florido is not only a point of entry but also a place imbued with historical significance. The border area has witnessed the ebb and flow of historical events that shaped the destinies of Guatemala and Mexico. Understanding the historical context is essential to appreciating the connections and influences that have shaped the cultures and societies of this region.

As travelers cross the El Florido border, they step into Chiapas—an enchanting Mexican state known for its diverse landscapes, indigenous communities, and rich cultural heritage. The

proximity of El Florido to Chiapas offers travelers access to experiences ranging from exploring the ancient ruins of Palenque to immersing themselves in the culinary delights of Chiapan cuisine.

The journey across El Florido is marked by diverse cultural encounters that provide a window into the shared traditions and unique identities of both Guatemala and Mexico. From sampling Guatemalan street food to savoring the flavors of Chiapan tamales, travelers experience a sensory journey that bridges culinary heritage.

El Florido's significance extends beyond its cultural offerings. The landscapes that envelop this border crossing are defined by their natural beauty, from the highland vistas of Guatemala to the lush rainforests and archaeological sites of Chiapas. This region beckons travelers to embark on explorations that extend beyond national borders.

At El Florido, the lines that separate countries blur as individuals from diverse backgrounds converge. The interactions between travelers, locals, and fellow explorers create a sense of shared humanity that transcends nationalities and unites people in the spirit of curiosity and connection.

With increased accessibility comes a responsibility to approach El Florido with respect and responsible tourism practices. By engaging with local communities, supporting local businesses, and valuing the environment, travelers contribute to the preservation of the authenticity and integrity of this border region.

El Florido border crossing is more than a point of entry; it's a threshold that invites travelers to engage with the rich cultural heritage, historical narratives, and natural wonders of Guatemala and Mexico. As individuals cross this border, they step into a realm where traditions merge, connections are forged, and shared experiences shape personal stories. Whether it's the bustling markets, the indigenous communities, or the diverse landscapes, El Florido encapsulates the essence of cross-cultural exploration and the beauty of human interaction across borders.

Agua Caliente – Honduras: A Pathway to Cross-Cultural Encounters

The Agua Caliente border crossing serves as a dynamic gateway that connects Guatemala and Honduras, facilitating the exchange of cultures, traditions, and experiences between these neighboring Central American nations. Nestled in the western part of Guatemala, this crossing

links the town of Esquipulas with Honduras' Copán department. More than a mere geographical juncture, Agua Caliente embodies the shared histories, vibrant communities, and the spirit of unity that bind Guatemala and Honduras together.

Agua Caliente holds a strategic position in the western highlands of Guatemala, near the town of Esquipulas. The border crossing provides an essential connection between these two countries, bridging the gap between the Guatemalan and Honduran cultures, landscapes, and ways of life.

At the heart of Agua Caliente's significance is its role as a crossroads of cultures. As travelers cross the border, they move between two nations with deep historical ties and a rich blend of indigenous heritage, colonial influences, and modern traditions. The interactions and intersections that occur at Agua Caliente create a vibrant mosaic that embodies the essence of Central American diversity.

The surrounding region is home to diverse indigenous communities that have shaped the cultural landscapes of both countries. The border crossing itself serves as a tribute to the enduring legacy of indigenous peoples in Central America. Travelers have the opportunity to engage with locals, learn about their traditional customs, and gain insights into their unique ways of life.

Agua Caliente has a history as a hub of trade and commerce, serving as a conduit for the movement of goods, ideas, and cultural exchanges. The border region reflects the economic interdependence between Guatemala and Honduras, as markets on both sides facilitate the flow of products and contribute to the livelihoods of local communities.

Agua Caliente is a place imbued with historical significance, as it has witnessed the ebb and flow of historical events that have shaped the destinies of both Guatemala and Honduras. Understanding the historical context provides travelers with a deeper appreciation of the connections and shared narratives that define the region.

Beyond the Agua Caliente border crossing lies the Copán department of Honduras—an area renowned for its archaeological treasures, natural beauty, and vibrant communities. The proximity to Copán offers travelers access to experiences ranging from exploring the ancient Mayan ruins of Copán to immersing themselves in the colorful markets and local cuisine.

The journey across Agua Caliente is marked by cultural discoveries that extend beyond national borders. From indulging in Guatemalan street food to savoring Honduran delicacies, travelers embark on a culinary adventure that reflects the cultural influences and flavors that have evolved over centuries.

Agua Caliente's significance extends to the natural beauty that surrounds it. From the highland landscapes of Guatemala to the scenic vistas and archaeological sites of Copán, this region invites travelers to embrace the spirit of exploration and venture beyond the boundaries of their home countries.

At Agua Caliente, the crossing of borders leads to the convergence of individuals from diverse backgrounds. The interactions between travelers, locals, and fellow explorers create a sense of shared humanity that transcends nationalities and fosters meaningful connections.

As the Agua Caliente border crossing becomes more accessible, there is a growing responsibility to approach it with respect and responsible tourism practices. Engaging with local communities, supporting local businesses, and appreciating the natural environment contribute to the preservation of the region's authenticity.

Agua Caliente border crossing is more than a point of transition; it's a juncture that beckons travelers to explore the rich cultural heritage, historical narratives, and natural wonders of Guatemala and Honduras. As individuals cross this border, they venture into a realm where cultures merge, stories unfold, and shared experiences shape the tapestry of human connection. Whether it's the bustling markets, the indigenous communities, or the diverse landscapes, Agua Caliente encapsulates the essence of cross-cultural encounters and the beauty of transcending borders.

Valle Nuevo – El Salvador: Embracing Authentic Encounters

The Valle Nuevo border crossing stands as a gateway that bridges the realms of Guatemala and El Salvador, allowing travelers to traverse landscapes, cultures, and experiences between these neighboring Central American nations. Situated in the western part of Guatemala, this border connects with El Salvador, offering a passage that transcends geographical boundaries to reveal the shared histories, natural wonders, and human connections that define the relationships between these countries.

Valle Nuevo occupies a strategic position where the highlands of Guatemala meet the landscapes of El Salvador. This border crossing serves as a portal that unites the Guatemalan town of Atescatempa with Valle Nuevo, providing a channel for cross-cultural interactions to flourish and for individuals to explore the treasures that both nations have to offer.

At the core of Valle Nuevo's significance lies its role as a canvas on which cultures converge. As travelers journey across the border, they are immersed in the experiences of two countries with distinct identities, yet interconnected histories. This convergence of Guatemalan and Salvadoran

cultures creates a vibrant tapestry that celebrates the region's diversity and the shared heritage that runs through its veins.

The surrounding region resonates with the echoes of indigenous heritage, as communities uphold their languages, traditions, and ways of life. The border crossing itself serves as a testament to the enduring legacy of Central America's indigenous peoples. Travelers are presented with a unique opportunity to engage with local residents, learn about their traditional customs, and gain insights into the contemporary expressions of their identities.

Valle Nuevo's historical role as a hub of trade and interaction continues to shape its significance today. The border region reflects the economic interdependence between Guatemala and El Salvador, as markets and cross-border exchanges contribute to the livelihoods of local communities on both sides.

Valle Nuevo is more than just a crossing point—it is a site imbued with historical narratives that have shaped the destinies of both nations. Understanding the historical context provides travelers with a deeper appreciation for the connections, cultural influences, and shared stories that have evolved over time.

Beyond the Valle Nuevo border crossing lies Chalatenango—a department in El Salvador renowned for its lush landscapes, historical sites, and welcoming communities. The proximity to Chalatenango offers travelers access to experiences that range from exploring the charming town of La Palma to hiking in the Montecristo Cloud Forest.

The journey across Valle Nuevo invites travelers to engage with the artistic expressions of both countries. From sampling Guatemalan street food to indulging in Salvadoran pupusas, travelers embark on a culinary adventure that reflects the cultural influences and flavors that have evolved over generations.

Valle Nuevo's significance extends beyond its cultural offerings to encompass the natural beauty that envelops the region. From the highland vistas of Guatemala to the pristine landscapes of Chalatenango, this area beckons travelers to embrace the spirit of exploration and venture beyond the boundaries of their home countries.

At Valle Nuevo, the crossing of borders leads to the convergence of individuals from diverse backgrounds. The interactions between travelers, locals, and fellow explorers foster a sense of shared humanity that transcends nationalities, fostering understanding and building bridges between cultures.

With accessibility to Valle Nuevo border crossing on the rise, there arises a responsibility to approach it with respect and responsible tourism practices. Engaging with local communities, supporting local businesses, and respecting the environment contribute to the preservation of the region's authenticity.

Valle Nuevo border crossing is not just a point of entry; it's a threshold that beckons travelers to delve into the rich cultural heritage, historical narratives, and natural splendors of Guatemala and El Salvador. As individuals traverse this border, they step into a realm where cultures merge, stories intertwine, and shared experiences shape the bonds that unite people. Whether it's the bustling markets, the indigenous communities, or the breathtaking landscapes, Valle Nuevo encapsulates the essence of cross-cultural encounters and the beauty of transcending borders.

Gracias a Dios – Belize: Connecting Borders, Celebrating Diversity

The Gracias a Dios border crossing serves as a gateway that links Guatemala and Belize, enabling travelers to traverse not only physical landscapes but also cultural nuances, histories, and the spirit of cross-cultural exploration. Nestled in the western highlands of Guatemala, this border crossing connects with Belize, offering a passage that transcends geographical boundaries to reveal the shared human connections, natural treasures, and historical legacies that bind these neighboring Central American nations.

Gracias a Dios occupies a pivotal position where the Guatemalan highlands merge with Belize's natural wonders. This border crossing stands as a symbolic portal that unites Guatemala's Melchor de Mencos with the Belizean town of Benque Viejo del Carmen, creating a conduit for travelers to embrace the beauty of both countries and engage in cross-cultural experiences.

At the heart of Gracias a Dios' significance lies its role as a meeting point for cultures. As travelers traverse this border, they embark on a journey that transcends national boundaries, entering a realm where two distinct identities—the Guatemalan and the Belizean—meld, intertwine, and create a tapestry of shared experiences and mutual understanding.

The surrounding region resonates with the echoes of indigenous heritage, as communities uphold their languages, traditions, and ways of life. The border crossing itself serves as a testament to the enduring legacy of the indigenous peoples of Central America. Travelers are presented with an extraordinary opportunity to engage with local residents, learn about their traditional customs, and gain insights into the contemporary expressions of their identities.

Historically a hub of trade and interaction, Gracias a Dios continues to foster economic exchanges that transcend national borders. The border region reflects the economic interdependence between Guatemala and Belize, as markets and cross-border exchanges contribute to the livelihoods of local communities on both sides.

Gracias a Dios is more than just a gateway—it is a site that has borne witness to historical events that have shaped the destinies of both nations. Understanding the historical context provides travelers with a deeper appreciation for the connections, cultural influences, and shared stories that have evolved over time.

Beyond the Gracias a Dios border crossing lies Belize—a nation renowned for its natural beauty, ancient Mayan ruins, and diverse ecosystems. The proximity to Belize opens a door to experiences that range from exploring the majestic ruins of Xunantunich to diving into the depths of the Blue Hole.

The journey across Gracias a Dios invites travelers to engage with the artistic expressions of both countries. From sampling Guatemalan street food to indulging in Belizean cuisine, travelers embark on a culinary journey that reflects the cultural influences and flavors that have evolved over generations.

Gracias a Dios' significance extends beyond cultural experiences to encompass the natural beauty that envelops the region. From the highland vistas of Guatemala to the pristine landscapes of Belize, this area beckons travelers to embrace the spirit of exploration and venture beyond the boundaries of their home countries.

At Gracias a Dios, the crossing of borders leads to the convergence of individuals from diverse backgrounds. The interactions between travelers, locals, and fellow explorers foster a sense of shared humanity that transcends nationalities, fostering understanding and building bridges between cultures.

With accessibility to the Gracias a Dios border crossing on the rise, there arises a responsibility to approach it with respect and responsible tourism practices. Engaging with local communities, supporting local businesses, and respecting the environment contribute to the preservation of the region's authenticity.

Gracias a Dios border crossing is not just a point of transition; it's a threshold that invites travelers to immerse themselves in the rich cultural heritage, historical narratives, and natural wonders of Guatemala and Belize. As individuals cross this border, they step into a realm where cultures merge, stories intertwine, and shared experiences shape the bonds that unite people. Whether it's the bustling markets, the indigenous communities, or the breathtaking landscapes, Gracias a Dios encapsulates the essence of cross-cultural encounters and the beauty of transcending borders.

Santa Elena – Belize: Bridging Cultures, Enriching Journeys

The Santa Elena border crossing stands as a gateway that seamlessly connects Guatemala and Belize, offering travelers a passage not only across geographical landscapes but also through the shared histories, diverse cultures, and natural wonders that define the relationships between these neighboring Central American nations. Nestled in the western highlands of

Guatemala, this border crossing extends an invitation to explore, understand, and appreciate the cross-cultural connections that thrive at the intersection of Santa Elena and Belize.

Santa Elena's geographical position marks the point where the rugged terrains of Guatemala converge with the lush landscapes of Belize. This border crossing serves as a symbolic doorway that unites Santa Elena in Guatemala with the Belizean town of San Ignacio, creating an avenue for travelers to traverse cultures, histories, and experiences that transcend national boundaries.

At the heart of Santa Elena's significance lies its role as a meeting ground for cultures. As travelers journey across the border, they step into a realm where Guatemalan and Belizean identities merge, resulting in a vibrant tapestry of shared experiences, mutual appreciation, and cross-cultural understanding.

The surrounding region resonates with the echoes of indigenous heritage, as communities uphold their languages, traditions, and ways of life. The border crossing itself serves as a tribute to the enduring legacy of the indigenous peoples of Central America. Travelers are presented with an opportunity to engage with local residents, learn about their traditional customs, and gain insights into the contemporary expressions of their identities.

Historically a center of trade and interactions, Santa Elena continues to foster economic exchanges that transcend national borders. The border region reflects the economic interdependence between Guatemala and Belize, as markets and cross-border exchanges contribute to the livelihoods of local communities on both sides.

Santa Elena is not just a gateway—it is a site that has witnessed historical events that have shaped the destinies of both nations. Understanding the historical context provides travelers with a deeper appreciation for the connections, cultural influences, and shared stories that have evolved over time.

Beyond the Santa Elena border crossing lies Belize—a nation renowned for its natural beauty, ancient Mayan ruins, and vibrant communities. The proximity to Belize opens the door to

experiences that range from exploring the mysterious Caracol ruins to embarking on a cave tubing adventure in the heart of the rainforest.

The journey across Santa Elena invites travelers to engage with the artistic expressions of both countries. From indulging in traditional Guatemalan street food to savoring Belizean cuisine, travelers embark on a culinary journey that reflects the cultural influences and flavors that have evolved over generations.

Santa Elena's significance extends beyond cultural immersion to encompass the natural beauty that envelops the region. From the highland vistas of Guatemala to the scenic landscapes of

Belize, this area encourages travelers to embrace the spirit of exploration and venture beyond the confines of their home countries.

At Santa Elena, the crossing of borders leads to the convergence of individuals from diverse backgrounds. The interactions between travelers, locals, and fellow explorers foster a sense of shared humanity that transcends nationalities, fostering understanding and forging bridges between cultures.

With the accessibility of the Santa Elena border crossing increasing, a responsibility arises to approach it with respect and responsible tourism practices. Engaging with local communities, supporting local businesses, and respecting the environment contribute to the preservation of the region's authenticity.

Santa Elena border crossing is more than a point of transition; it's a threshold that beckons travelers to immerse themselves in the rich cultural heritage, historical narratives, and natural wonders of Guatemala and Belize. As individuals traverse this border, they step into a realm where cultures intertwine, stories converge, and shared experiences shape the bonds that unite people. Whether it's the bustling markets, the indigenous communities, or the breathtaking landscapes, Santa Elena encapsulates the essence of cross-cultural encounters and the beauty of transcending borders.

San Cristóbal – Mexico: A Portal to Cultural Exploration

The San Cristóbal border crossing serves as a passage that connects Guatemala and Mexico, providing travelers with an avenue to experience the convergence of cultures, histories, and landscapes between these two neighboring nations. Nestled in the heart of Central America, this border crossing is more than a geographical intersection—it's a gateway to uncovering the

shared connections, vibrant traditions, and cross-cultural encounters that define the relationship between San Cristóbal and both countries.

San Cristóbal occupies a strategic position where the highlands of Guatemala meet the enchanting landscapes of Mexico. This border crossing serves as a symbolic bridge that links the Guatemalan town of La Mesilla with the Mexican town of La Trinitaria, opening up a pathway for travelers to explore diverse cultures, histories, and experiences that transcend national boundaries.

At the heart of San Cristóbal's significance lies its role as a crossroads of cultures. As travelers journey across this border, they traverse between two nations that share histories, yet each possess unique identities and traditions. The interaction between Guatemalan and Mexican cultures creates a vibrant tapestry that highlights the beauty of diversity and the power of shared human connections.

The surrounding region echoes with the rich heritage of indigenous communities, who have preserved their languages, rituals, and ways of life. The border crossing itself stands as a tribute to the enduring legacy of indigenous peoples in Central America and Mexico. Travelers have the opportunity to engage with local residents, learn about their traditional customs, and gain insights into their contemporary expressions of identity.

San Cristóbal's historical role as a hub of trade and economic interaction continues to shape its significance. The border region reflects the economic interdependence between Guatemala and Mexico, as markets and cross-border exchanges contribute to the livelihoods of local communities on both sides.

San Cristóbal is not merely a point of entry—it is a site that has witnessed historical events that have shaped the destinies of both nations. Understanding the historical context provides travelers with a deeper appreciation for the connections, cultural influences, and shared narratives that have evolved over time.

Beyond the San Cristóbal border crossing lies the Mexican state of Chiapas—a region renowned for its captivating landscapes, indigenous communities, and vibrant cultural heritage. The proximity to Chiapas offers travelers access to experiences that range from exploring the colonial charm of San Cristóbal de las Casas to immersing themselves in the natural wonders of Sumidero Canyon.

The journey across San Cristóbal invites travelers to immerse themselves in the artistic expressions of both countries. From savoring traditional Guatemalan dishes to indulging in the flavors of Mexican cuisine, travelers embark on a culinary adventure that reflects the cultural influences and flavors that have evolved over generations.

San Cristóbal's significance extends to the breathtaking landscapes that surround it. From the highland vistas of Guatemala to the picturesque scenery of Chiapas, this region beckons travelers to embrace the spirit of exploration and venture beyond the confines of their home countries.

At San Cristóbal, the crossing of borders leads to the convergence of individuals from diverse backgrounds. The interactions between travelers, locals, and fellow explorers create a sense of shared humanity that transcends nationalities, fostering understanding and building bridges between cultures.

As accessibility to the San Cristóbal border crossing increases, a responsibility arises to approach it with respect and responsible tourism practices. Engaging with local communities, supporting local businesses, and respecting the environment contribute to the preservation of the region's authenticity.

The San Cristóbal border crossing is not just a juncture; it's an invitation to delve into the rich cultural heritage, historical narratives, and natural wonders of Guatemala and Mexico. As individuals cross this border, they step into a realm where cultures merge, stories intertwine, and shared experiences shape the bonds that unite people. Whether it's the bustling markets, the indigenous communities, or the captivating landscapes, San Cristóbal encapsulates the essence of cross-cultural encounters and the beauty of transcending borders.

Section 4: Top Destinations in Guatemala

Guatemala is a country rich in natural beauty, ancient history, and vibrant culture. Whether you're interested in exploring ancient Mayan ruins, immersing yourself in colorful indigenous markets, or enjoying breathtaking landscapes, Guatemala has something for every type of traveler. Here are some of the best top destinations in Guatemala that you won't want to miss:

1. Antigua Guatemala: This UNESCO World Heritage site is a colonial gem with cobblestone streets, colorful buildings, and stunning architecture. Explore its historic churches, convents, and ruins, and soak in the atmosphere of this charming city surrounded by volcanoes.

2. Tikal: Located in the heart of the jungle, Tikal is one of the most iconic Mayan archaeological sites in the world. Climb ancient pyramids, explore temples, and imagine the bustling city that once thrived here.

3. Lake Atitlán: Surrounded by towering volcanoes, Lake Atitlán is a picturesque destination known for its beauty and tranquility. Explore the villages along the lakeshore, each with its own distinct culture and traditions.

4. Chichicastenango: This town is famous for its vibrant indigenous market, where you can shop for handmade crafts, textiles, and traditional goods. The market is a feast for the senses and a window into Guatemala's rich cultural heritage.

5. Quetzaltenango (Xela): The second-largest city in Guatemala, Xela is known for its Spanish language schools and its proximity to hot springs, hiking trails, and the Fuentes Georginas thermal pools.

6. Semuc Champey: This natural wonder consists of a series of limestone pools and waterfalls set amidst lush jungle. It's a paradise for nature lovers and adventurers.

7. Livingston: Accessible only by boat, Livingston is a unique Caribbean town with a distinct Garifuna culture. Enjoy the laid-back atmosphere, delicious seafood, and reggae rhythms.

8. Monterrico: If you're looking for beach time, Monterrico offers black sand beaches along the Pacific coast. It's also a nesting ground for sea turtles, making it a popular spot for wildlife enthusiasts.

9. Rio Dulce: A tropical paradise with lush landscapes and the tranquil Rio Dulce river flowing through it. Explore the river, visit hot springs, and discover the stunning Lake Izabal.

10. Nebaj: For a more off-the-beaten-path experience, visit Nebaj in the highlands. This town is a gateway to indigenous villages, traditional weaving, and stunning mountain scenery.

11. Peten Region: Apart from Tikal, the Peten region has more to offer, including the lesser-known Mayan sites of Yaxha and El Mirador, as well as the abundant wildlife of the Maya Biosphere Reserve.

12. Izabal Region: Visit the picturesque town of Livingston, explore the historic Castillo de San Felipe, and relax on the shores of Lake Izabal.

13. Cobán: Nestled in the cloud forests of the Alta Verapaz region, Cobán is known for its lush landscapes, waterfalls, and coffee plantations. Don't miss the stunning Semuc Champey, a series of turquoise pools and natural limestone bridges.

14. Salcajá: This small town is home to the oldest church in Central America, the Church of San Jacinto. The church's history and architectural significance make it a must-visit for history enthusiasts.

15. Huehuetenango:Located in the highlands near the border with Mexico, Huehuetenango offers stunning mountain views, vibrant markets, and the opportunity to learn about the indigenous Mam culture.

16. Retalhuleu: Home to the popular theme park Xetulul and the water park Xocomil, Retalhuleu is a family-friendly destination where you can enjoy rides, shows, and water activities.

17. Jutiapa: Known for its beautiful landscapes, Jutiapa offers a mix of natural attractions, including El Baúl hill, Las Peñitas Lake, and the El Jute Ecological Park.

18. Monjas: This small town is famous for its colorful murals that depict local history and culture. The murals add a unique artistic touch to the streetscape.

19. Pacaya Volcano: For adventure seekers, a hike up Pacaya Volcano offers the chance to see volcanic activity up close and even roast marshmallows on the lava rocks.

20. Acatenango Volcano: Another popular volcano for hiking, Acatenango offers stunning views of neighboring Fuego Volcano's eruptions and a breathtaking sunrise.

21. Chiquimula: This department is known for its diverse landscapes, including the Caves of Loltún, the Agua Caliente hot springs, and the ancient Mayan site of Quiriguá.

22. Esquipulas: Visit the Basilica of Esquipulas, a pilgrimage site famous for the Black Christ statue. The town is an important religious and cultural hub.

23. El Mirador: For adventurers seeking a more remote experience, El Mirador is a challenging trek that leads to one of the largest Mayan archaeological sites, hidden deep in the jungle.

24. Iximché: Explore the archaeological ruins of Iximché, a former capital of the Kaqchikel Maya. The site offers insight into pre-Columbian history and architecture.

25. Barrio de San Felipe: In Antigua, this neighborhood is known for its colorful buildings and colonial charm. It's a wonderful place to wander and immerse yourself in the local ambiance.

These destinations offer just a glimpse into the incredible diversity that Guatemala has to offer. From ancient ruins and vibrant markets to lush landscapes and active volcanoes, this country invites travelers to explore, discover, and appreciate the rich tapestry of its culture and natural beauty.

Antigua Guatemala: A Journey Through Time and Culture

Nestled in the heart of the Guatemalan highlands, Antigua Guatemala stands as a living testament to the convergence of history, culture, and beauty. This UNESCO World Heritage site captivates visitors with its cobblestone streets, colonial architecture, and vibrant atmosphere. Beyond its picturesque façade lies a rich tapestry of stories, traditions, and experiences that have shaped the city's identity and made it one of the most beloved destinations in Central America.

As one steps into Antigua, time seems to shift, transporting visitors to a bygone era. Founded in 1543 as Santiago de los Caballeros, the city served as the capital of the Spanish colonial Captaincy General of Guatemala for over two centuries. Throughout its history, Antigua experienced a series of earthquakes, volcanic eruptions, and political changes that left their mark on its architecture, culture, and character.

The colonial architecture that graces the streets of Antigua is a visual testament to its illustrious past. Rows of colorful buildings adorned with intricate facades, wooden balconies, and ornate churches create a scene that is reminiscent of a well-preserved painting from centuries past. From the iconic Santa Catalina Arch to the majestic La Merced Church, each structure tells a story of resilience and adaptation in the face of nature's forces.

Antigua's history is deeply intertwined with its religious identity. The city boasts an astonishing number of churches, each with its own unique history and significance. Ruins of grand cathedrals stand as silent witnesses to the earthquakes that reshaped the cityscape. Iglesia y Convento de las Capuchinas, a former convent turned museum, offers insights into the lives of cloistered nuns and their devotion.

Antigua is a place where traditions come alive. The city pulses with the energy of its people, who actively participate in rituals, celebrations, and cultural practices that have been passed down through generations. Semana Santa (Holy Week) is a prime example, during which elaborate processions and alfombras (colored sawdust carpets) transform the streets into a living canvas of devotion and creativity.

The city's creative spirit is embodied in its artisans, who produce intricate textiles, ceramics, and crafts that reflect the vibrancy of Guatemalan culture. The bustling markets offer visitors the chance to engage with local artisans, learn about their techniques, and take home one-of-a-kind souvenirs that carry a piece of Antigua's soul.

Antigua's allure extends beyond its physical beauty. The city has become a hub for language learners from around the world, drawn to its numerous Spanish language schools. Immersing oneself in the language while exploring the city's enchanting corners creates a unique educational and cultural experience.

Antigua's culinary scene is a fusion of traditional Guatemalan flavors and international influences. From bustling street food markets to elegant dining establishments, the city offers a gastronomic journey that tempts the taste buds and showcases the diversity of Guatemalan cuisine.

While steeped in history, Antigua is also surrounded by stunning natural landscapes. The towering Agua, Fuego, and Acatenango volcanoes provide a breathtaking backdrop, and adventurous travelers can embark on hikes to their summits for spectacular sunrise views.

As Antigua's popularity as a tourist destination grows, so does the responsibility to preserve its cultural and historical heritage. Efforts to promote sustainable tourism, support local businesses, and protect the city's architectural gems are crucial to ensuring that future generations can continue to experience the magic of Antigua.

Antigua Guatemala is more than a city; it's a living canvas that captures the essence of time, culture, and human connection. Its cobblestone streets, colonial facades, and vibrant traditions intertwine to create an experience that transcends the ordinary and transports visitors to a world where past and present coexist in harmony. As travelers explore its enchanting corners, engage with its people, and immerse themselves in its stories, they become part of the intricate fabric of Antigua's narrative, leaving with memories that will forever tie them to this remarkable city.

Tikal: Unveiling the Majesty of Ancient Mayan Civilization

In the heart of the Guatemalan jungle, Tikal stands as a testament to the ingenuity, grandeur, and mystique of the ancient Mayan civilization. This archaeological wonder, hidden amidst the dense foliage of the Petén region, beckons travelers on a journey through time, where monumental pyramids, intricate temples, and a rich history come together to offer a glimpse into a civilization that flourished over a thousand years ago.

Tikal's story is one of rediscovery. For centuries, its towering structures lay concealed beneath layers of vegetation, their true significance known only to the local indigenous populations. It wasn't until the late 19th century that explorers and archaeologists began to unveil the secrets that lay beneath the jungle's embrace, revealing a city that once thrived as a cultural, political, and religious epicenter.

At the heart of Tikal's allure are its monumental architectural achievements. The towering pyramids, ornate temples, and intricate plazas tell a story of a civilization that was both technologically advanced and deeply attuned to the cosmos. Structures like Temple I and Temple II reach skyward, offering panoramic views of the surrounding jungle canopy, while the awe-inspiring Temple IV stands as a sentinel, providing a vantage point to witness sunrise and sunset over the treetops.

The Mayans' connection to the cosmos is deeply ingrained in Tikal's layout and architecture. The city's alignment with celestial events, such as solstices and equinoxes, demonstrates the Mayans' intricate understanding of astronomy and their reverence for the natural world. Observatories like El Caracol served as centers for studying the stars and tracking celestial cycles.

Tikal was more than a collection of buildings; it was a hub of culture, trade, and intellectual exchange. Its plazas, ball courts, and hieroglyphic inscriptions offer insights into the rituals, ceremonies, and daily life of the Mayan people. The Great Plaza, surrounded by temples and pyramids, served as a central gathering place for civic and religious events.

Tikal's history is woven with the stories of its rulers—kings and queens who governed the city and left their mark in the form of stelae, altars, and tombs. The Great Jaguar Paw, Jasaw Chan K'awiil I, and Lady Twelve Macaw are among the influential figures whose legacies are carved into the stone structures, preserving their memory for generations to come.

Tikal is not only a treasure trove of archaeological wonders but also a haven for biodiversity. The surrounding rainforest is home to a variety of wildlife, including howler monkeys, toucans, and jaguars. The juxtaposition of ancient ruins and thriving ecosystems adds to Tikal's enchantment, creating a harmonious blend of history and nature.

For modern-day explorers, Tikal offers a unique blend of archaeological exploration and adventure. Hiking through the jungle trails that connect the different sites allows travelers to experience the environment much as the ancient Mayans did. The sounds of the forest, the rustling leaves, and the occasional glimpse of wildlife create an immersive journey through time.

As Tikal's popularity as a tourist destination grows, there is a heightened responsibility to preserve its cultural heritage and natural surroundings. Sustainable tourism practices, including guided tours, restricted access to certain areas, and conservation efforts, are crucial to maintaining the integrity of this archaeological marvel for future generations.

Tikal's significance extends beyond its historical and architectural wonders; it serves as a bridge that connects us to the ingenuity, spirituality, and complex society of the ancient Mayans. As travelers stand before the towering pyramids and immerse themselves in the aura of the jungle, they become part of a lineage that spans centuries. Tikal invites us to contemplate the passage of time, the resilience of cultures, and the enduring allure of human achievement.

Tikal stands as a beacon of human achievement, a monument to the past that continues to inspire awe and wonder in the present. It is a place where history, nature, and human curiosity converge, inviting us to explore the mysteries of an ancient civilization and connect with the rhythms of the natural world. Tikal's pyramids, temples, and plazas are not mere structures; they are windows into a world that thrived long ago, a world that still has much to teach us about the boundless potential of human creativity and imagination.

Lake Atitlán: A Jewel of Nature and Culture

Nestled within the embrace of towering volcanoes and lush hills, Lake Atitlán is a shimmering jewel that captures the hearts of travelers with its breathtaking beauty and rich cultural tapestry. Known as the "Jewel of the Highlands," this stunning lake in the Guatemalan highlands is more than just a geographical wonder—it's a destination that invites exploration, introspection, and immersion into the vibrant traditions and landscapes that define its allure.

Lake Atitlán's beauty is a symphony of natural elements that come together to create a harmonious tableau. Formed within the caldera of a massive ancient volcano, the lake's crystal-clear waters reflect the majestic peaks that encircle it. Three towering volcanoes—Atitlán,

Tolimán, and San Pedro—stand as sentinels, their slopes adorned with verdant forests and coffee plantations that spill down to meet the shoreline.

For the indigenous Mayan communities that have called the Lake Atitlán region home for centuries, the lake holds deep cultural and spiritual significance. It is believed to be a place where the material and spiritual worlds intersect, with each of its volcanoes representing one of the Mayan deities. This sacred connection infuses the lake's atmosphere with a sense of reverence and tranquility.

Lake Atitlán's shores are dotted with a series of charming villages, each with its own distinct character and traditions. Panajachel, often the gateway to the lake, offers a blend of local markets and artisan shops where visitors can purchase intricately woven textiles and handcrafted goods. Santiago Atitlán, with its vibrant markets and indigenous traditions, provides a window into contemporary Mayan life.

The villages surrounding Lake Atitlán provide a window into the enduring traditions of the Mayan people. Visitors have the opportunity to engage with local communities, witness traditional ceremonies, and learn about the art of weaving, pottery, and other crafts that have been passed down through generations.

Lake Atitlán is not just a place to admire from a distance—it's a playground for adventurers and nature enthusiasts. Hiking trails wind through the hills, offering stunning panoramic views of the lake and the surrounding landscape. Those seeking a more challenging experience can embark on the ascent of San Pedro Volcano, rewarded with sweeping vistas from its summit.

The lake itself is a playground for water-based activities. Kayaking, paddleboarding, and boat tours offer the chance to explore its pristine waters and discover hidden coves and villages. Relaxing boat rides provide a unique perspective of the lake's beauty, allowing travelers to soak in the tranquility and capture picturesque moments.

Lake Atitlán has inspired artists, writers, and creators for generations. Its serene beauty and captivating landscapes offer a canvas for artistic expression. Visitors can immerse themselves in the local art scene, where galleries and studios showcase works influenced by the lake's natural splendor and cultural heritage.

As Lake Atitlán becomes increasingly popular, the importance of sustainable tourism practices becomes paramount. Efforts to protect the lake's ecosystem, promote responsible waste disposal, and support local initiatives are essential to ensuring that the beauty of Lake Atitlán remains unspoiled for future generations.

Lake Atitlán's ethereal beauty and tranquil ambiance create an environment conducive to reflection and renewal. The lake's serene shores provide a sanctuary for introspection, meditation, and a reconnection with nature. As the sun dips below the horizon and the stars emerge, travelers can revel in a sense of wonder that transcends the boundaries of time and space.

Lake Atitlán is more than a geographic wonder—it's a living testament to the interplay between nature and culture, a place where the sacred and the sublime converge. It invites travelers to embark on a journey that transcends the ordinary and immerses them in the rhythms of life that have echoed across its shores for centuries. As one gazes upon its shimmering waters and contemplates the majesty of the surrounding landscape, they become part of the narrative of Lake Atitlán—a story of beauty, spirituality, and the enduring connection between humanity and the natural world.

Chichicastenango: A Tapestry of Colors, Culture, and Tradition

Nestled high in the Guatemalan highlands, the town of Chichicastenango emerges like a vibrant tapestry woven from the threads of centuries-old traditions, indigenous culture, and the bustling energy of local markets. Known affectionately as "Chichi" by both locals and travelers, this small town is a captivating destination that offers a window into the heart of Guatemala's rich cultural heritage. From its bustling markets to its historic churches, Chichicastenango beckons visitors to immerse themselves in its colors, sounds, and timeless traditions.

Chichicastenango's history is interwoven with the tapestry of Mayan civilization, Spanish colonial influence, and contemporary indigenous life. As one of the largest indigenous communities in Central America, the town remains a stronghold of the Mayan K'iche' culture, preserving ancient customs that have endured the test of time.

The heartbeat of Chichicastenango resonates most vibrantly in its bustling markets. On Thursdays and Sundays, the town's streets transform into a vibrant mosaic of colors, as vendors gather to sell an array of goods that reflect the diversity and creativity of Guatemala's artisans. From intricately woven textiles to handmade pottery, vibrant masks, and traditional clothing, the market is a treasure trove of authentic craftsmanship.

At the center of Chichicastenango stands the iconic Santo Tomás Church, a testament to the intersection of indigenous beliefs and Catholicism. This historic church, built atop the remnants of a pre-Columbian temple, represents the fusion of Mayan spirituality and colonial influence. Visitors can witness the unique blend of rituals and ceremonies that take place both within the church and on its steps, where offerings and incense intertwine with Catholic symbolism.

Chichicastenango's spiritual essence extends beyond the church walls. The town's indigenous inhabitants maintain a deep connection to their ancestral beliefs, and rituals are woven into daily life. Visitors may encounter Mayan priests conducting ceremonies in the central plaza, invoking blessings for health, success, and harmony.

Just a short walk from the central plaza lies the Pascual Abaj ritual site, a sacred place where locals pay homage to their spiritual heritage. The site features an altar adorned with offerings and candles, a testament to the continuing vitality of indigenous beliefs in the face of changing times.

Chichicastenango's authenticity extends beyond its markets and rituals to its quaint streets and neighborhoods. The town's colonial architecture, narrow cobblestone streets, and red-tiled roofs create an ambiance that transports visitors to another era. The local workshops and stores offer an opportunity to observe artisans at work, producing goods that echo the town's rich artistic heritage.

Colors have a profound significance in Chichicastenango. The vibrant huipiles (traditional blouses) worn by the women of the town are not merely clothing; they are expressions of identity, heritage, and a connection to the land. Each pattern, motif, and color holds meaning, telling stories of the wearer's community and life journey.

Chichicastenango's culinary scene is a feast for the senses. The aromas of traditional Guatemalan cuisine waft through the air, drawing visitors to market stalls and street vendors. From hearty stews to savory tamales, the town's cuisine offers a delectable journey through the flavors of Guatemala.

Chichicastenango's significance transcends its physical attributes; it's a place where community thrives and connections are forged. The town's warmth and hospitality make visitors feel like honorary participants in its vibrant tapestry of life. Engaging with locals, sharing stories, and learning about their daily experiences offer travelers a deeper understanding of the town's heart and soul.

Chichicastenango's ability to preserve its cultural heritage while embracing modernity is a testament to its resilience and adaptability. The town's indigenous identity remains strong even as it engages with contemporary challenges and opportunities.

Chichicastenango invites travelers on a journey that transcends the boundaries of time and space. It's a journey that celebrates the enduring spirit of a community, the artistry of its people, and the profound beauty of its traditions. As visitors wander through the bustling markets, stand before the Santo Tomás Church, and connect with the vibrant energy that courses through the town, they become part of Chichicastenango's ongoing story—a story of culture, tradition, and the timeless threads that bind us all.

Quetzaltenango (Xela): Where Culture, History, and Nature Converge

Nestled within the highlands of Guatemala, Quetzaltenango, affectionately known as Xela, emerges as a city that seamlessly weaves together a rich tapestry of history, culture, and natural beauty. As the country's second-largest city, Xela stands as a dynamic hub where traditions are preserved, language is studied, and the scenic landscapes of the Western Highlands captivate the hearts of those who venture to its enchanting streets.

Xela's roots stretch deep into history, where its origins trace back to pre-Columbian times. Established by the Mam people, Xela has a legacy that encompasses indigenous heritage, Spanish colonization, and modernization. As a city with a vibrant past, Xela's streets, plazas, and architecture tell tales of transformation, adaptation, and the interplay between cultures.

The Mam people continue to be an integral part of Xela's identity, and their cultural presence is felt throughout the city. Indigenous textiles, traditional clothing, and the use of the Mam language serve as reminders of the enduring heritage that shapes Xela's character. The city becomes a portal to engage with indigenous traditions, offering travelers a glimpse into the customs and daily life of the Mam community.

Xela's cobblestone streets are often filled with the sounds of students immersed in language studies. The city's reputation as a language-learning destination has attracted individuals from around the world seeking to improve their Spanish skills. Language schools offer an immersive experience, enabling visitors to interact with locals, practice their language abilities, and delve into the cultural nuances that enrich communication.

Xela's architectural diversity reflects its historical journey. Colonial-era buildings adorned with intricate facades stand as a testament to Spanish influence, while indigenous elements intertwine seamlessly with modern constructions. The Iglesia del Espíritu Santo and the Catedral de San Juan provide glimpses into the city's spiritual and architectural heritage.

Plazas serve as the heart of Xela, where community life unfolds against a backdrop of picturesque landscapes. The Parque Centro América offers a space for leisurely strolls, interactions, and cultural events. Markets and stalls dot the plazas, showcasing artisan crafts, fresh produce, and local goods that represent the diverse facets of Guatemalan life.

Xela's role as a commercial center is a testament to its vitality. Markets, both traditional and modern, bustle with activity, reflecting the city's role in trade and commerce. The Mercado

Central is a focal point where locals and visitors alike can explore a kaleidoscope of products, from textiles to spices, and experience the vibrant pulse of Xela's economic life.

Surrounded by stunning landscapes, Xela offers a gateway to explore the natural wonders of the Western Highlands. The nearby Santa María and Santiaguito volcanoes present opportunities for challenging hikes and rewarding panoramic views. The Fuentes Georginas hot springs provide relaxation amidst the misty mountain air, while the scenic Laguna Chicabal offers a serene oasis for reflection.

Xela's calendar is punctuated by cultural festivities that celebrate the city's history and heritage. The Feria de Independencia in September pays homage to Guatemala's independence, while Semana Santa brings about elaborate processions, intricate alfombras (sawdust carpets), and religious ceremonies that engage both locals and visitors.

Xela's warm and welcoming atmosphere creates a sense of community that resonates with travelers. The city's vibrant culture invites visitors to interact with locals, partake in cultural activities, and share experiences that forge connections and lasting memories.

As Xela's popularity grows, the importance of sustainable tourism practices becomes increasingly evident. Efforts to protect the city's historical and cultural heritage, promote responsible tourism, and support local initiatives contribute to the preservation of Xela's authenticity and vibrancy.

Xela isn't just a destination—it's an embodiment of Guatemala's intricate cultural fabric and a reflection of the country's past, present, and future. As travelers traverse its streets, engage with its people, and embrace its landscapes, they become part of the narrative that Xela weaves—a story of diversity, heritage, and the unending evolution of a city that bridges cultures and generations. Whether it's the echoes of indigenous traditions, the rhythm of language studies, or the breathtaking vistas of the Highlands, Xela invites us to explore, learn, and immerse ourselves in its captivating embrace.

Semuc Champey: Nature's Hidden Oasis of Beauty and Adventure

Nestled deep within the lush jungles of Guatemala, Semuc Champey stands as a breathtaking natural wonder that captivates the senses and ignites the spirit of adventure. This hidden gem, tucked away in the heart of the Alta Verapaz region, is a paradise of turquoise pools, cascading waterfalls, and verdant landscapes. As travelers venture into this remote oasis, they are rewarded with an unparalleled blend of pristine beauty, outdoor exploration, and a connection to the raw power of nature.

Semuc Champey is an awe-inspiring creation of nature, born from the convergence of the Cahabón River and the limestone hills that surround it. The result is a series of stepped pools carved into the rock, each pool a brilliant shade of turquoise. These natural infinity pools form a staircase-like formation, with cascading water flowing between them, creating a visual spectacle that seems almost surreal.

Semuc Champey's allure isn't limited to passive admiration; it beckons travelers to embrace adventure and immerse themselves in its beauty. Exploration of the site includes traversing a series of trails that lead to viewpoints offering breathtaking vistas of the pools below. Visitors can also venture down to the water's edge, where they can swim, wade, and experience the cool, crystal-clear waters up close.

One of the highlights of a visit to Semuc Champey is the K'anba Cave experience. Equipped with a candle and guided by local experts, visitors venture into the depths of the cave, wading through underground rivers and traversing narrow passageways. The experience is an exhilarating blend of adrenaline and wonder, as travelers navigate the darkness and emerge into chambers adorned with shimmering stalactites and stalagmites.

Semuc Champey isn't just a feast for the eyes; it's also a playground for outdoor enthusiasts. The surrounding landscape offers a range of activities, from hiking through dense jungles to exploring nearby waterfalls and natural springs. The adventurous can engage in tubing down the Cahabón River, where the gentle current carries them through vibrant landscapes and offers a unique perspective on the area's natural beauty.

The serene beauty of Semuc Champey isn't just about adventure—it's also a place of tranquility and rejuvenation. Visitors find solace in the rhythmic sound of flowing water, the dappled sunlight filtering through the trees, and the cool embrace of the pools. Whether it's meditating by the water's edge or simply taking in the sights and sounds, Semuc Champey offers a unique opportunity for introspection and relaxation.

Semuc Champey's remote location underscores the importance of responsible tourism and environmental preservation. Efforts to minimize the impact of visitors and promote sustainable practices are essential to ensuring that this natural marvel remains unspoiled for generations to come. Local initiatives focused on conservation, waste management, and education contribute to the preservation of the area's ecological balance.

Semuc Champey serves as a reminder of the raw power and beauty of nature, reminding us of our place within the intricate web of life on Earth. Its serene pools, rushing waterfalls, and vibrant flora and fauna evoke a sense of wonder and humility, inviting us to connect with the natural world in ways that awaken our senses and remind us of the importance of stewardship.

Visiting Semuc Champey is more than a travel experience; it's a journey of connection, discovery, and awe. As travelers navigate its trails, swim in its pools, and explore its hidden corners, they become part of a narrative that spans millennia—a narrative of the Earth's transformative power and the enduring beauty it creates. Semuc Champey invites us to step off the beaten path, embrace the unknown, and immerse ourselves in a world of unparalleled beauty and adventure.

Livingston: A Cultural Haven Where the Caribbean Meets Guatemala

Nestled on the northeastern coast of Guatemala, Livingston emerges as a vibrant and unique destination where the rich tapestry of Caribbean culture mingles with the traditions of the Guatemalan highlands. This picturesque town, accessible only by boat, is a haven for travelers seeking a different side of Guatemala—an enchanting blend of Afro-Caribbean rhythms, Garífuna heritage, and the beauty of the tropical coastline. With its laid-back ambiance, colorful streets, and deep-rooted cultural diversity, Livingston beckons explorers to immerse themselves in an experience that transcends borders and encompasses the soul of two worlds.

To arrive in Livingston is to step into a world apart from the rest of Guatemala. The town's isolation, surrounded by lush jungle and bounded by the Caribbean Sea, has preserved its unique cultural identity and character. The town's distinctiveness is immediately evident in its architecture, music, cuisine, and the warm hospitality of its people

Central to the heart of Livingston is its Garífuna community, descendants of West African, Arawak, and Carib peoples who settled in the region centuries ago. The Garífuna culture is a celebration of resilience, creativity, and a deep connection to the sea. Drum rhythms, traditional dances, and vibrant music reflect a heritage that is proudly preserved and shared with visitors.

The flavors of Livingston's cuisine tell the story of its cultural fusion. Garífuna dishes, often prepared with coconut, fish, and plantains, are a testament to the town's Afro-Caribbean roots. Visitors can savor the unique taste of hudut (fish stew), tapado (seafood soup), and cassava bread while gaining insight into the culinary traditions that have been passed down through generations.

Livingston's coastal location offers a gateway to the natural wonders of the Caribbean. The surrounding waters are teeming with marine life, making it a haven for snorkeling and diving enthusiasts. Nearby Siete Altares is a series of cascading waterfalls and natural pools that provide a refreshing respite from the tropical heat.

Livingston's allure extends beyond Garífuna culture. The town's atmosphere is enriched by the presence of Maya Q'eqchi' communities, further adding to its cultural mosaic. Visitors can witness the interplay of languages, traditions, and customs as they explore the streets and interact with the diverse population.

Punta Gorda, a short boat ride away, serves as a connection between Guatemala and Belize. Travelers seeking to extend their exploration can venture to this coastal town in Belize, where a different Caribbean experience awaits. The blending of cultures, languages, and landscapes continues in Punta Gorda, offering an opportunity for cross-cultural exchange.

Livingston's atmosphere of tranquility and simplicity makes it an ideal place to unwind and escape the hustle of modern life. The pace is slower, the surroundings idyllic, and the gentle waves of the Caribbean provide a soothing backdrop. It's a place where hammocks sway in the breeze, inviting visitors to embrace the art of doing nothing.

Livingston's cultural diversity creates an environment of exchange and understanding. Visitors have the chance to learn about the traditions, history, and daily life of both the Garífuna and Maya Q'eqchi' communities. Engaging with locals, sharing stories, and participating in cultural activities contribute to meaningful interactions that go beyond tourism.

As tourism grows in Livingston, the importance of responsible travel practices becomes increasingly evident. Efforts to support local initiatives, respect cultural traditions, and contribute to environmental conservation are essential to ensuring that the town's unique character and natural beauty remain intact.

Livingston's charm lies in its ability to unite two worlds—the vibrancy of the Caribbean and the rich heritage of Guatemala. It's a place where music, language, food, and traditions intertwine to create an experience that is unlike any other. As visitors explore its colorful streets, dance to the rhythms of its music, and savor its culinary delights, they become part of the harmony that Livingston embodies—a harmony that celebrates diversity, fosters connections, and reveals the beauty of cultures interwoven.

Monterrico: Where Beaches, Mangroves, and Sea Turtles Unite

Nestled along the Pacific coast of Guatemala, Monterrico emerges as a coastal paradise that beckons travelers with its pristine beaches, vibrant mangroves, and a deep connection to the sea turtles that grace its shores. This idyllic town, set against the backdrop of volcanic landscapes and the azure Pacific Ocean, offers a unique blend of relaxation, natural beauty, and wildlife conservation. Monterrico's unspoiled beaches, rich biodiversity, and commitment to preserving its unique ecosystem make it a destination that invites visitors to embrace the tranquility of the coast while contributing to the protection of its precious inhabitants.

Monterrico serves as a gateway to the Pacific, offering a serene escape from the bustle of everyday life. Its tranquil beaches, characterized by volcanic black sand and gentle waves, create an environment of relaxation and rejuvenation. Whether it's basking in the sun, strolling along the shoreline, or listening to the soothing rhythm of the waves, Monterrico provides a refuge for those seeking to unwind.

Monterrico's natural beauty extends beyond its beaches to the intricate ecosystems of mangroves and wetlands that flourish in the area. These biodiverse environments are home to a myriad of plant and animal species, providing a haven for birdwatching, kayaking, and explorations that reveal the interconnectedness of coastal life.

One of Monterrico's most significant features is its role in sea turtle conservation. The town's beaches serve as nesting grounds for several species of sea turtles, including the olive ridley, leatherback, and hawksbill turtles. Guided turtle tours offer visitors the chance to witness the awe-inspiring sight of these ancient creatures coming ashore to lay their eggs, a spectacle that underscores the delicate balance between human activity and the preservation of wildlife.

Monterrico's commitment to sea turtle conservation is evident through the establishment of turtle hatcheries. These efforts provide a safe haven for turtle eggs, protecting them from predators and poachers. As the hatchlings emerge from their nests, they are released into the ocean, a poignant reminder of the town's dedication to nurturing the delicate cycle of life in the ocean.

Monterrico is surrounded by nature reserves that showcase the area's biodiversity and offer opportunities for outdoor exploration. The Hawaii Nature Reserve, for instance, is a lush habitat for birdwatching and observing the native flora and fauna. The reserves offer guided tours and interpretive walks that provide insights into the region's unique ecosystems.

Monterrico's Pacific-facing position grants visitors the privilege of witnessing stunning sunsets over the ocean. The sky transforms into a canvas of fiery hues, casting a mesmerizing glow over the water. The town's proximity to volcanic landscapes adds to its allure, as travelers can catch glimpses of nearby volcanoes on the horizon.

Monterrico's charm is enhanced by the warmth of its local community. Visitors have the opportunity to interact with locals, learn about their customs and way of life, and partake in cultural activities. This engagement contributes to a deeper understanding of the town's essence and fosters connections that go beyond the surface.

As tourism in Monterrico grows, so does the importance of responsible travel practices. Efforts to minimize the impact on the environment, support local initiatives, and contribute to conservation efforts are essential to ensuring that the town's natural beauty and wildlife thrive for generations to come.

Monterrico is more than a coastal destination; it's a symphony of life that resonates with the rhythms of the sea, the whispering of the mangroves, and the ancient journey of sea turtles. It's a place where the ebb and flow of nature's cycles intersect with the efforts of a community committed to safeguarding its precious inhabitants. As travelers embrace the tranquility of its beaches, explore its wetlands, and bear witness to the magic of sea turtles returning to the sea, they become part of a story that celebrates the beauty of life on Earth and the vital role each one of us plays in its conservation. Monterrico invites us to savor the moment, cherish the natural world, and leave behind footprints of connection and care.

Rio Dulce: Navigating the Waters of Tranquility and Discovery

Nestled within the lush landscapes of Guatemala, Rio Dulce emerges as a haven of natural beauty, historic intrigue, and waterborne exploration. This picturesque region, where the tranquil river winds its way through dense jungles, offers travelers a unique opportunity to immerse themselves in a journey that unveils the diverse facets of Central America. From the vibrant flora and fauna that thrive along its banks to the captivating blend of indigenous culture and colonial history, Rio Dulce invites adventurers to navigate its waters and uncover the stories that have shaped its identity.

At the heart of Rio Dulce's allure is its eponymous river, a serpentine waterway that meanders through verdant landscapes and tropical rainforests. The river's calm waters and lush

surroundings create an atmosphere of tranquility and serenity, providing an idyllic setting for exploration and introspection.

The journey along Rio Dulce leads to Lake Izabal, the largest lake in Guatemala. The lake's expansive waters provide ample opportunities for boating, fishing, and soaking in the natural beauty that envelops the region. Moreover, the river eventually connects with the Caribbean Sea, opening up a maritime passage that has shaped the region's history and culture.

The landscapes that flank Rio Dulce's waters are teeming with biodiversity. From the resplendent plumage of tropical birds to the playful antics of monkeys swinging through the trees, the region's wildlife offers a symphony of sights and sounds that underscore the importance of environmental conservation.

As Rio Dulce flows into Lake Izabal, it creates an ecosystem that is home to the endangered West Indian manatee. The area is designated as a manatee sanctuary, and travelers may be fortunate enough to catch glimpses of these gentle creatures as they surface for air. The sanctuary's presence is a testament to the region's commitment to protecting its unique inhabitants.

Perched atop a hill overlooking Rio Dulce, the Castillo de San Felipe de Lara stands as a testament to the region's colonial past. This Spanish fortress, dating back to the 17th century, was strategically built to defend against pirates and foreign invasions. Exploring the castle's stone walls, cannons, and commanding views transports visitors to a time when the river played a pivotal role in protecting the region.

The region around Rio Dulce is inhabited by indigenous communities that have maintained their cultural heritage and connection to the land. Visitors have the opportunity to engage with locals, witness traditional ceremonies, and gain insights into the customs and way of life that define their identity.

Beyond its riverbanks, Rio Dulce's surroundings offer a range of natural wonders to explore. The hot springs of Finca Paraiso provide a relaxing respite, where visitors can soak in the therapeutic waters while surrounded by lush greenery. The Biotopo Chocón Machacas, a protected area, is home to a diverse array of flora and fauna, inviting hikers and nature enthusiasts to discover its hidden treasures.

Exploring Rio Dulce often involves navigating its waters, whether by boat, kayak, or canoe. Travelers can embark on guided river tours that showcase the region's natural beauty, cultural heritage, and historical significance. As the boat glides through the river's gentle currents, passengers are treated to panoramic views of the surrounding landscapes.

As Rio Dulce gains popularity as a travel destination, the importance of responsible tourism practices becomes paramount. Efforts to support local communities, minimize environmental impact, and contribute to conservation initiatives are crucial to preserving the region's natural beauty and cultural authenticity.

Rio Dulce is more than a geographical feature; it's a river of stories that intertwine nature, history, and human connection. It's a place where the past and present converge, where tranquil waters carry with them the echoes of indigenous traditions and colonial legacies. As travelers navigate its currents, explore its landscapes, and engage with its people, they become part of the narrative that Rio Dulce weaves—a narrative of exploration, discovery, and the enduring spirit of a region where water has shaped not only the physical landscape but also the hearts and minds of those who call it home.

Nebaj: Unveiling the Heart of the Ixil Triangle

Nebaj, a town nestled in the highlands of Guatemala, emerges as a place of resilience, cultural richness, and a profound connection to the land. Situated within the Ixil Triangle, an area that was deeply affected by Guatemala's civil conflict, Nebaj stands as a testament to the enduring spirit of its indigenous inhabitants. With its vibrant markets, colorful textiles, and awe-inspiring landscapes, Nebaj invites travelers to delve into its history, explore its traditions, and witness the transformative power of community.

The history of Nebaj is intertwined with the tumultuous events that unfolded during Guatemala's civil conflict, a period marked by violence and displacement. The town's resilience, however, shines through as its people continue to rebuild their lives and preserve their cultural identity. Nebaj's journey from adversity to resurgence is a story of strength and hope that inspires those who visit.

Nebaj is at the heart of the Ixil region, inhabited by the indigenous Ixil Maya people. The town and its surroundings offer an immersion into Ixil culture, where customs, language, and traditions are cherished and shared. Visitors have the opportunity to engage with locals, witness traditional ceremonies, and gain insights into the way of life that has endured for generations.

The town's bustling markets are a reflection of its vibrant cultural tapestry. Market days are a sensory delight, with the streets coming alive as vendors sell colorful textiles, handmade crafts, fresh produce, and traditional foods. The markets offer an authentic glimpse into the daily life of the Ixil people and provide an opportunity to support local artisans.

Nebaj is renowned for its intricate textiles, which serve as a visual expression of cultural identity and ancestral heritage. Women play a pivotal role in preserving the art of traditional weaving, creating garments adorned with intricate patterns that convey stories of the community's history and spirituality.

Spirituality is deeply ingrained in the fabric of Nebaj's community. The town is dotted with churches that blend Catholicism with indigenous beliefs, creating a unique syncretic expression of faith. Visitors may encounter rituals, ceremonies, and celebrations that honor both traditional practices and Catholic traditions.

Nebaj's surroundings are characterized by the awe-inspiring beauty of the highland landscapes. The Cuchumatanes mountain range, with its misty peaks and verdant valleys, creates a stunning backdrop that invites exploration. Hiking trails, pristine lakes, and opportunities for outdoor adventure abound, allowing travelers to immerse themselves in the natural wonders of the region.

Efforts to preserve Nebaj's historical memory are evident in initiatives such as community museums and cultural centers. These spaces offer insights into the town's history, struggles, and triumphs, allowing visitors to gain a deeper understanding of the challenges faced by its people and the strides they have made towards healing and empowerment.

Nebaj's cuisine is a reflection of the land's bounty and the fusion of cultural influences. Traditional dishes often incorporate locally grown ingredients, creating a harmony of flavors that celebrate the region's agricultural heritage. Sharing a meal with locals provides an opportunity to savor the tastes of Nebaj and connect with the people who call it home.

Nebaj's commitment to education is a testament to its aspirations for the future. The town is home to schools and initiatives that provide educational opportunities for children, empowering them to pursue knowledge and shape their own destinies. Education serves as a bridge between generations, fostering a sense of hope and possibility.

Visiting Nebaj is more than a travel experience; it's a journey of connection and exchange. Engaging with the people, participating in cultural activities, and sharing stories create bonds that transcend language barriers and cultural differences. Through these interactions, travelers become part of Nebaj's ongoing narrative—a narrative of resilience, cultural pride, and the unwavering spirit of a community that has faced challenges with courage and determination.

Nebaj unveils the beauty of humanity in its rawest form. It's a place where the echoes of history resound, where traditions are celebrated, and where the landscape mirrors the strength and endurance of its people. As visitors traverse its streets, engage with its inhabitants, and marvel at its landscapes, they become part of Nebaj's story—a story that is both a tribute to the past and a testament to the future, a story of a town that embodies the power of culture, community, and the indomitable human spirit.

Peten Region: Exploring the Heart of the Maya World

Nestled in the northern reaches of Guatemala, the Peten Region emerges as a captivating realm that invites travelers to journey into the heart of the ancient Maya civilization. This expansive and biodiverse region is a tapestry of history, culture, and natural wonders, where ancient ruins rise from the jungle canopy, wildlife thrives in protected reserves, and the legacy of the Maya people lives on in the present day. From the majestic temples of Tikal to the tranquil waters of Lake Peten Itza, the Peten Region is a landscape of exploration and discovery that bridges the gap between the past and the present.

Peten is often regarded as the cradle of Maya civilization, as it was home to some of the most significant cities of the ancient Maya world. The region's dense jungles once concealed sprawling cities that thrived for centuries, their impressive architecture and intricate hieroglyphs a testament to the advanced culture that flourished here.

The jewel of the Peten Region is undoubtedly Tikal, an ancient Maya city that stands as a UNESCO World Heritage Site and a window into the past. Towering pyramids, grand plazas, and intricate stelae transport visitors to an era when Tikal was a vibrant center of culture, trade, and ceremonial significance. Climbing to the top of one of Tikal's pyramids offers panoramic views of the surrounding jungle, where the calls of howler monkeys and the rustling of leaves create a symphony of the wild.

While Tikal may be the most famous, it's not the only archaeological wonder in Peten. El Mirador, often referred to as the "Lost City of the Maya," is a remote site that has captivated archaeologists and adventurers alike. Its massive structures, including the Danta pyramid, provide insights into the complexity and grandeur of Maya urban centers.

Yaxha, located near the shores of Lake Yaxha, is another archaeological treasure in the Peten Region. The city's temples and pyramids rise above the water's edge, creating a mesmerizing reflection in the calm lagoons that surround it. Exploring Yaxha's plazas and structures offers a glimpse into the Maya world and the intricate network of settlements that once thrived here.

Lake Peten Itza, a serene and picturesque body of water, provides a tranquil escape from the archaeological marvels of the region. Surrounded by lush forests and dotted with islands, the lake offers opportunities for boating, fishing, and relaxation. The charming town of Flores, situated on an island in the lake, serves as a gateway to both the water and the cultural attractions of the Peten Region.

Peten's diverse ecosystems support an array of wildlife, making it a haven for nature enthusiasts. The region is home to numerous protected areas and wildlife reserves, including

the Maya Biosphere Reserve, one of the largest protected areas in Central America. Here, jaguars, tapirs, and a variety of bird species thrive in their natural habitats, creating opportunities for wildlife spotting and ecological exploration.

The Maya Biosphere Reserve encompasses not only archaeological sites but also diverse landscapes, including wetlands, tropical forests, and savannas. Efforts to protect both cultural heritage and biodiversity make this reserve a prime example of the symbiotic relationship between nature and history.

Peten is not only a repository of ancient history but also a place where the legacy of the Maya people lives on. Indigenous communities maintain their traditions, language, and way of life, providing visitors with a chance to engage with local culture through markets, ceremonies, and interactions with community members.

Exploring the culinary offerings of the Peten Region reveals a blend of traditional Maya ingredients and flavors with modern influences. Dishes such as pepián (a hearty stew) and atole (a traditional drink) showcase the region's culinary heritage, while international influences are evident in the vibrant food scene of towns like Flores.

As the Peten Region gains recognition as a travel destination, the importance of responsible tourism practices becomes evident. Efforts to support local communities, minimize environmental impact, and contribute to conservation initiatives are crucial to preserving the natural beauty, cultural authenticity, and historical significance of the region.

The Peten Region is more than a geographical expanse; it's a journey through time and nature, a voyage that uncovers the layers of history that shape its identity. It's a place where the echoes of ancient rituals mingle with the rustling of leaves, where the grandeur of ancient cities stands as a testament to human achievement, and where the biodiversity of protected reserves reminds us of the interconnectedness of all life.

Exploring the Peten Region is an invitation to unravel the mysteries of the Maya world, to witness the resilience of indigenous communities, and to bask in the beauty of its natural landscapes. As visitors traverse its archaeological sites, navigate its lakes, and engage with its people, they become part of the narrative that Peten weaves—a narrative of exploration, connection, and the enduring legacy of a region that holds the secrets of both the ancient and the contemporary Maya civilizations.

Izabal Region: Where Nature and History Converge in Harmony

Nestled along the northeastern shores of Guatemala, the Izabal Region unfurls as a captivating tapestry of natural beauty, historical intrigue, and a rich blend of cultures. From the serene waters of Lake Izabal to the lush landscapes of national parks, Izabal invites travelers to embark on a journey that bridges the gap between the ancient Maya civilization and the vibrant traditions of modern-day communities. With its colonial towns, archaeological sites, and lush rainforests, Izabal is a realm of exploration where the echoes of history resonate and the vibrant spirit of Guatemala comes to life.

At the heart of the Izabal Region lies Lake Izabal, the largest lake in Guatemala. Its expansive waters stretch out in a mesmerizing panorama, reflecting the lush greenery that surrounds it. The lake serves as a playground for water activities, such as boating, fishing, and kayaking, offering an opportunity to connect with the tranquility of nature.

Nestled along the Caribbean coast of Lake Izabal, Livingston emerges as a vibrant hub of Garífuna culture. The town's Afro-Caribbean roots are evident in its music, dance, and cuisine. Visitors to Livingston have the chance to immerse themselves in the rhythms of the Caribbean, savor traditional dishes, and witness the blending of cultures that define this unique coastal community.

On the shores of Lake Izabal, the Castillo de San Felipe de Lara stands as a sentinel of history. This colonial fortress, built by the Spanish to protect against pirate attacks, evokes the region's past as a strategic maritime crossroads. Exploring its stone walls and admiring its views of the lake, visitors are transported to an era of colonial struggles and maritime exploration.

Flowing from Lake Izabal is the Rio Dulce, a majestic river that winds its way through lush rainforests and dense mangroves. The river serves as a gateway to Lake Izabal, offering a tranquil journey that unveils the region's natural splendor. Navigating the Rio Dulce is a serene experience, allowing travelers to immerse themselves in the rich ecosystems that thrive along its banks.

Venturing beyond the shores of Lake Izabal, travelers encounter Quirigua, an ancient Maya archaeological site that offers insights into the civilization's history and architectural prowess. The site's intricately carved stelae and monuments stand as silent witnesses to the achievements of the past. Quirigua's UNESCO World Heritage status underscores its significance as a portal to the Maya world.

The natural beauty of the Izabal Region extends to the Cerro San Gil National Park, a protected area characterized by lush rainforests, diverse flora, and abundant wildlife. Hiking through its trails provides an opportunity to encounter the region's biodiversity, including tropical birds, howler monkeys, and vibrant plant life.

El Boqueron National Park is another gem within the Izabal Region, offering a haven for nature enthusiasts and adventure seekers. The park's waterfalls, rivers, and hiking trails beckon visitors to explore its hidden corners, and its natural pools provide a refreshing respite from the tropical heat.

The Izabal Region's cultural diversity is a reflection of its history as a crossroads of trade and migration. Indigenous communities, Garífuna populations, and the influence of Spanish colonization have all contributed to the region's cultural mosaic. Engaging with locals, participating in traditional ceremonies, and exploring local markets provide opportunities for cultural immersion and connection.

Izabal's culinary offerings celebrate the bounty of both land and water. Fresh seafood, tropical fruits, and local ingredients infuse dishes with vibrant flavors and a hint of the Caribbean. Savoring the region's cuisine is an invitation to indulge in the tastes that define Izabal's cultural identity.

As the Izabal Region gains recognition as a travel destination, efforts to preserve its natural beauty and cultural heritage become paramount. Conservation initiatives, sustainable tourism practices, and local engagement are essential to ensuring that the region's ecosystems and traditions thrive for generations to come.

Izabal is more than a geographical region; it's a journey through time and landscape, a passage that unravels the threads of history and the wonders of nature. It's a place where ancient ruins tell stories of a distant past, where the melodies of Caribbean music merge with indigenous traditions, and where the rhythms of life flow alongside the tranquil waters of Lake Izabal.

Exploring the Izabal Region is an immersion in a symphony of diversity, where the echoes of Maya rituals, colonial struggles, and Garífuna rhythms harmonize in the present day. As travelers navigate its waters, uncover its archaeological treasures, and engage with its people, they become part of the narrative that Izabal weaves—a narrative of connection, discovery, and the vibrant tapestry of a region that celebrates the harmonious blend of nature and culture.

Cobán: Exploring the Enchanted Heart of Guatemala

Nestled in the verdant highlands of Guatemala, Cobán emerges as a captivating destination that enchants travelers with its lush landscapes, vibrant culture, and unique blend of indigenous traditions and colonial heritage. This charming town, surrounded by mist-covered mountains and fertile valleys, invites visitors to embark on a journey that delves into the heart of Guatemala's cultural tapestry. From its vibrant markets to its picturesque waterfalls, Cobán beckons explorers to uncover the stories that shape its identity and experience the beauty of its natural and cultural wonders.

Cobán is situated in the heart of the Alta Verapaz region, an area known for its striking beauty and abundant vegetation. The town's elevation ensures a mild and pleasant climate, making it a haven for those seeking respite from the heat of the lowlands. As travelers arrive in Cobán, they are greeted by the embrace of cool mountain air and a landscape that seems to have sprung from the pages of a storybook.

Cobán is home to a diverse population, with indigenous communities playing a significant role in shaping its cultural fabric. The Q'eqchi' Maya people have a strong presence in the region, preserving their traditions, language, and way of life. As visitors explore the town and its surroundings, they have the opportunity to witness the interplay of indigenous customs and colonial influences that have left an indelible mark on the area.

Cobán's markets are a vibrant reflection of its cultural tapestry. Market days are a feast for the senses, with stalls brimming with fresh produce, colorful textiles, handmade crafts, and traditional foods. The markets offer a window into the daily life of the Q'eqchi' Maya and provide visitors with a chance to engage with local artisans and support their craftsmanship.

One of the highlights of Cobán's cultural calendar is Semana Santa, or Holy Week. This religious celebration draws visitors from far and wide to witness processions, ceremonies, and festivities that reflect the deep spiritual beliefs of the community. The streets come alive with colorful carpets made from sawdust and flowers, creating a visual spectacle that resonates with both locals and visitors.

Cobán's natural beauty extends beyond its town center to the surrounding landscapes. The region is adorned with a collection of breathtaking waterfalls, each with its own unique charm. From the cascades of El Salto de Chilascó to the hidden gem of El Biotopo del Quetzal, these natural wonders provide opportunities for hiking, photography, and a deep connection with the land.

The Biotopo del Quetzal, a protected natural reserve, is a sanctuary for one of Guatemala's most iconic and elusive birds—the resplendent quetzal. This vibrant bird, revered by the Maya civilization, finds refuge in the lush cloud forests of the reserve. Birdwatchers and nature enthusiasts can immerse themselves in the enchanting melodies of the forest and catch glimpses of this magnificent creature in its natural habitat.

The vicinity of Cobán offers an opportunity for cave exploration, with the Lanquin Caves being a notable highlight. Venturing into the depths of these caves unveils a world of subterranean formations, including stalactites and stalagmites, that evoke a sense of wonder and mystery.

Cobán's commitment to ecotourism and sustainability is evident in its efforts to protect its natural heritage. The Biotopo del Quetzal and other reserves reflect the region's dedication to conservation and responsible tourism practices. Engaging with these initiatives not only allows travelers to experience the beauty of the land but also contributes to its preservation.

Cobán is known for its coffee plantations, which produce some of Guatemala's finest brews. Exploring the coffee estates offers insights into the process of cultivation, harvesting, and roasting that bring this beloved beverage to life. Coffee enthusiasts can savor the flavors of locally grown beans and learn about the integral role coffee plays in the region's economy and culture.

Cobán is a living testament to the rich cultural tapestry that defines Guatemala. It's a place where ancient traditions and modern influences intermingle, where the rhythms of indigenous music echo through the streets, and where the aroma of coffee wafts through the air. As visitors traverse its markets, engage with its people, and explore its natural wonders, they become part of Cobán's narrative—a narrative that celebrates diversity, preserves heritage, and invites connection.

Exploring Cobán is a journey of enchantment, where misty mountains, ancient customs, and the allure of the unknown beckon travelers to uncover its treasures. It's a place where the rustling of leaves and the calls of birds harmonize with the stories of the past and the hopes of the present. As travelers traverse its landscapes, engage with its communities, and embrace its traditions, they become part of Cobán's enchanting tale—a tale of discovery, authenticity, and the unending beauty of a region that captures the heart and ignites the imagination.

Salcajá: Tracing History in Guatemala's Timeless Town

Nestled among the lush landscapes of Guatemala, the small town of Salcajá emerges as a hidden gem that whispers tales of history, spirituality, and cultural significance. With its

cobblestone streets, colonial architecture, and a deeply rooted connection to indigenous traditions, Salcajá offers travelers a glimpse into the past and a chance to witness the threads that weave together the tapestry of Guatemala's diverse heritage. As visitors meander through its streets, explore its landmarks, and engage with its warm-hearted inhabitants, they embark on a journey of discovery that transcends time and space.

Salcajá is renowned for its colonial charm, with architecture that harks back to a bygone era. The town's cobblestone streets and white-washed facades create an atmosphere of antiquity, inviting visitors to step into the pages of history. The Church of San Jacinto, one of Salcajá's most iconic landmarks, stands as a testament to colonial craftsmanship, with its intricate façade and centuries-old bell tower.

The Church of San Jacinto, built in the 16th century, is a living repository of history and faith. It is known for its distinct architectural style, which blends Spanish colonial influences with indigenous elements. The church's significance goes beyond its aesthetic appeal—it serves as a spiritual hub where locals gather to celebrate their faith and maintain a connection to their cultural heritage.

Salcajá holds a unique claim to fame as the home of the first distillery in Central America. Established in 1755, this distillery produced the region's first rum, marking a historical milestone that resonates with the town's legacy of innovation and craftsmanship. The distillery's legacy lives on, reminding visitors of the ingenuity that shaped the region's cultural and economic landscape.

Salcajá's significance goes beyond its colonial heritage—it's also a place where indigenous traditions thrive. The town is inhabited by the Quiché Maya people, who continue to honor their spiritual beliefs and practices. Visitors may have the opportunity to witness traditional ceremonies, encounter shamans, and gain insights into the spiritual fabric that binds the community.

Textile artistry is deeply embedded in Salcajá's cultural identity. The town is known for its weaving traditions, where artisans create vibrant textiles adorned with intricate patterns and designs. The art of weaving serves as a bridge between generations, preserving the knowledge and techniques that have been passed down through the ages.

Salcajá's market days are a vibrant reflection of local life and cultural exchange. The markets burst with colors as vendors showcase fresh produce, handcrafted goods, and traditional foods. Engaging with locals in this lively setting provides a glimpse into the daily rhythms of the town and offers the chance to savor authentic flavors.

Beyond textiles, Salcajá is home to a community of artisans who create an array of handicrafts. From ceramics to woodwork, these artisans infuse their creations with a blend of tradition and

innovation. Exploring their workshops and galleries allows visitors to witness the dedication and skill that define Salcajá's artistic landscape.

Visiting Salcajá is an invitation to engage in cultural exchange and connection. The town's warm and welcoming inhabitants often greet visitors with open arms, sharing stories, traditions, and a sense of community that transcends language barriers and cultural differences. Through these interactions, travelers become part of Salcajá's ongoing narrative—a narrative of heritage, spirituality, and the unbreakable bonds of humanity.

Salcajá is more than a picturesque town; it's a journey through time and identity, a passage that unveils layers of history and cultural significance. It's a place where cobblestone streets echo with footsteps from centuries past, where the whispers of ancient ceremonies resonate, and where the vibrant hues of textiles mirror the vibrant spirit of its people.

Salcajá stands as a testament to resilience, celebrating the enduring spirit of a community that has preserved its heritage amidst the currents of change. It's a town where the echoes of the past harmonize with the pulse of the present, inviting travelers to embrace the stories etched into its streets and immerse themselves in the beauty of a destination that captures the essence of Guatemala's rich and diverse heritage.

Retalhuleu: Where History and Nature Embrace

Nestled in the southwestern reaches of Guatemala, Retalhuleu emerges as a captivating destination that weaves together a rich tapestry of history, culture, and natural beauty. This charming town, situated between the Pacific Ocean and the towering Sierra Madre mountain range, invites travelers to embark on a journey of exploration that uncovers the stories of ancient civilizations, celebrates the traditions of modern-day communities, and immerses visitors in the lush landscapes that define the region. From its archaeological sites to its vibrant festivals, Retalhuleu offers an authentic glimpse into the soul of Guatemala.

Retalhuleu is situated in a region of remarkable diversity, where coastal plains meet mist-shrouded mountains. The town's location makes it a gateway to both Pacific beaches and mountain retreats, offering a range of experiences that cater to all types of travelers. The landscapes surrounding Retalhuleu are as varied as they are breathtaking, providing a canvas of natural beauty that sets the stage for exploration.

One of Retalhuleu's most significant archaeological sites is Tak'alik Ab'aj, often referred to as the "Hill of the Stone Writing." This site is an archaeological treasure trove that unveils the history of ancient civilizations, including the Olmec and Maya cultures. Stelae, altars, and intricate

sculptures provide insights into the spiritual beliefs and artistic expressions of the past, allowing visitors to step back in time and connect with the legacies of these ancient societies.

Retalhuleu boasts a colonial heritage that is evident in landmarks such as the San Felipe Castle. This colonial-era fortress, perched on a hill overlooking the town, stands as a symbol of the town's history and the struggles of its past. Exploring the castle's stone walls and admiring its panoramic views allows visitors to trace the footsteps of those who shaped the region's destiny.

Retalhuleu's cultural vibrancy is celebrated through a calendar of festivals and events that showcase the town's traditions and spirit. From religious processions to lively fiestas, these gatherings offer visitors an opportunity to immerse themselves in the local culture and witness the convergence of indigenous customs and colonial influences.

For those seeking a tranquil escape, the Amatitlán Lagoon provides a serene oasis surrounded by lush greenery. The lagoon's calm waters offer opportunities for boating, kayaking, and relaxation. As the sun sets over the water, the lagoon becomes a place of reflection and rejuvenation.

Retalhuleu's proximity to the Pacific coast makes it an ideal starting point for beach excursions. The town's accessibility to renowned beach destinations, such as Champerico and Monterrico, offers travelers the chance to bask in the sun, ride the waves, and savor the flavors of coastal cuisine.

Retalhuleu invites travelers to engage in cultural exchange and connection, fostering interactions with locals that transcend language barriers and cultural differences. Engaging with the warm-hearted inhabitants allows visitors to learn about daily life, traditions, and the strong sense of community that defines the region.

Artisans in Retalhuleu continue to uphold the traditions of craftsmanship, creating intricate textiles, pottery, and other handicrafts that reflect the town's cultural identity. Exploring workshops and interacting with artisans offers a firsthand experience of the creativity and skill that define Retalhuleu's artistic landscape.

Retalhuleu's commitment to conservation is reflected in its efforts to protect the region's natural wonders. Nearby national parks and protected areas provide habitats for diverse flora and fauna, allowing travelers to immerse themselves in the beauty of the natural world while contributing to its preservation.

Retalhuleu is a living fusion of the past and the present, a town where ancient ruins stand side by side with colonial landmarks, and where traditions are woven into the fabric of daily life. As visitors traverse its landscapes, engage with its inhabitants, and participate in its cultural events, they become part of Retalhuleu's ongoing narrative—a narrative that celebrates heritage,

embraces diversity, and beckons travelers to experience the authenticity that defines this charming corner of Guatemala.

Exploring Retalhuleu is an authentic experience that uncovers the layers of history, embraces the rhythm of local life, and showcases the stunning landscapes that encompass the town. It's a journey that offers insights into the resilience of past civilizations and the enduring spirit of modern communities. As travelers immerse themselves in Retalhuleu's culture, connect with its people, and appreciate its natural wonders, they become part of a timeless narrative that captures the essence of Guatemala's diverse and captivating soul.

Jutiapa: Exploring the Charms of Eastern Guatemala

Nestled in the southeastern corner of Guatemala, Jutiapa emerges as a destination that blends natural beauty, cultural richness, and a strong sense of community. This captivating region, characterized by rolling hills, fertile valleys, and charming towns, invites travelers to embark on a journey that unravels the stories of its past, celebrates its present, and showcases the landscapes that define its identity. From its historic landmarks to its vibrant festivals, Jutiapa offers an authentic experience that captures the essence of Guatemala's diverse heritage and the enduring spirit of its people.

Jutiapa's landscape is a testament to the region's diversity. The region's topography varies from lush valleys to rugged mountains, creating a tapestry of natural beauty that captivates the eye.

The town's proximity to the Pacific coast further adds to its appeal, providing a range of experiences that cater to all types of travelers.

One of Jutiapa's most significant historical sites is Quiriguá, an ancient Maya city that stands as a testament to the civilization's architectural prowess and cultural significance. The site's intricately carved stelae and monuments offer insights into the Maya world, allowing visitors to step back in time and marvel at the achievements of this ancient civilization.

Jutiapa is also home to charming colonial towns that reflect the region's rich history. As travelers stroll through cobblestone streets and admire colonial architecture, they are transported to an era of Spanish influence and colonial legacy. These towns offer a glimpse into the past and a chance to connect with the communities that have preserved their cultural heritage.

Jutiapa's cultural richness is celebrated through a calendar of festivals and events that showcase the town's traditions and spirit. From vibrant fiestas to religious processions, these gatherings provide visitors with the opportunity to engage with the local culture, witness traditional customs, and connect with the warm-hearted inhabitants.

Jutiapa is not only steeped in history but also adorned with natural wonders. The region boasts a collection of picturesque waterfalls, each with its own unique charm. From the cascades of El Chorro de la Concepción to the tranquil beauty of El Aguacate waterfall, these natural treasures invite travelers to hike, photograph, and immerse themselves in the splendor of the outdoors.

The fertile lands of Jutiapa are the heart of the region's agricultural activities. The region's agricultural traditions are deeply woven into its cultural fabric, with farming playing a central role in the livelihoods of the local communities. Engaging with locals and witnessing traditional farming practices offers insights into the region's connection to the land.

Artisans in Jutiapa continue to uphold traditional craftsmanship, creating textiles, ceramics, and other handicrafts that reflect the town's cultural identity. Visitors can explore workshops, interact with artisans, and gain a deeper appreciation for the creativity and skill that define Jutiapa's artistic landscape.

Jutiapa invites travelers to embrace community connection and warmth, fostering interactions with locals that transcend language barriers and cultural differences. Engaging with the town's inhabitants offers a firsthand experience of the spirit of hospitality and the strong sense of unity that define the region.

Jutiapa's commitment to conservation is evident in its efforts to protect its natural and cultural heritage. The region's protected areas and reserves provide habitats for diverse flora and fauna, allowing travelers to experience the beauty of nature while contributing to its preservation.

Jutiapa is a living fusion of the past and the present, a place where ancient ruins coexist with colonial landmarks, and where traditions are an integral part of daily life. As travelers traverse its landscapes, engage with its communities, and immerse themselves in its cultural events, they become part of Jutiapa's ongoing narrative—a narrative that celebrates heritage, embraces diversity, and beckons visitors to experience the authenticity that defines this corner of Guatemala.

Exploring Jutiapa is an authentic journey that peels back the layers of history, embraces the rhythms of local life, and uncovers the natural beauty that envelops the town. It's a voyage that pays homage to the resilience of past civilizations and the enduring spirit of modern communities. As travelers immerse themselves in Jutiapa's culture, connect with its people, and appreciate its landscapes, they become part of a narrative that captures the heart and soul of Guatemala's diverse and captivating essence.

Monjas: Discovering Tranquility in Guatemala's Hidden Gem

Nestled in the heart of the Jalapa department of Guatemala, the small town of Monjas offers a serene escape that captivates travelers with its untouched beauty, charming simplicity, and a genuine connection to the land and its people. Far away from the bustling cities and tourist hotspots, Monjas invites visitors to step into a world where time seems to stand still, where the rhythms of daily life are intertwined with nature's harmony, and where the spirit of community flourishes. From its lush landscapes to its warm-hearted inhabitants, Monjas beckons explorers to uncover the treasures of a destination that captures the essence of Guatemala's tranquil and authentic soul.

Monjas is a haven of tranquility, surrounded by rolling hills, verdant valleys, and the timeless embrace of nature. The town's location away from the main tourist circuits contributes to its unspoiled charm, making it a retreat for those seeking respite from the fast pace of modern life. As travelers arrive in Monjas, they are welcomed by a sense of serenity that permeates the air and invites them to embrace the unhurried rhythm of the town.

Monjas is characterized by its strong sense of community, where neighbors know one another by name and visitors are welcomed as friends. The warmth of the inhabitants creates an atmosphere of hospitality that fosters genuine connections. Engaging with the locals offers an opportunity to witness the authenticity of daily life, share stories, and immerse oneself in the welcoming embrace of Monjas' residents.

The region's agricultural heritage plays a central role in the lives of Monjas' inhabitants. As visitors traverse the landscapes, they encounter fields of crops, coffee plantations, and traditional farming practices that have been passed down through generations. Engaging with locals and learning about their agricultural traditions provides insights into the connection between the land and the livelihoods of the community.

Monjas is home to skilled artisans who practice traditional crafts and create handmade goods that reflect the town's cultural identity. From intricate textiles to intricate woodwork, these creations are a testament to the region's creativity and craftsmanship. Exploring workshops and interacting with artisans allows visitors to gain a deeper appreciation for the skill and dedication that define Monjas' artistic landscape.

The natural beauty of Monjas invites exploration and appreciation. The surrounding landscapes are adorned with lush vegetation, coffee farms, and breathtaking viewpoints that offer panoramic vistas of the region's undulating hills. Hiking through these trails provides an

opportunity to connect with nature, discover hidden corners, and capture the essence of the outdoors.

Monjas' cultural identity is celebrated through festivals and events that reflect the town's traditions and spirit. From religious processions to community fiestas, these gatherings offer visitors a chance to witness the convergence of indigenous customs and community bonds. Participating in these celebrations provides an immersive experience of Monjas' cultural richness.

Monjas' relationship with nature is profound and enduring. The town's inhabitants have maintained a close connection to the land, incorporating the rhythms of the natural world into their daily lives. This connection is reflected in the town's traditions, practices, and the respect shown to the environment that sustains the community.

As travelers engage with the town and its inhabitants, they contribute to Monjas' sustainable practices and eco-tourism initiatives. These efforts aim to preserve the region's natural beauty, cultural heritage, and traditional way of life for future generations. Engaging in responsible tourism allows visitors to be a part of the conservation and preservation of this hidden gem.

Monjas is a testament to the beauty of simplicity and authenticity. It's a place where the rustling of leaves and the songs of birds replace the noise of the urban world, where genuine smiles and heartfelt conversations take precedence over screens and devices. As travelers immerse themselves in the town's rhythms, engage with its inhabitants, and embrace its tranquil landscapes, they become part of Monjas' ongoing narrative—a narrative of connection, authenticity, and the timeless beauty that defines this hidden corner of Guatemala.

Exploring Monjas is an unforgettable journey that reveals the essence of Guatemala's rural life, celebrates the bonds of community, and offers a glimpse into the heart of the land. It's a voyage that honors the traditions of the past and the dreams of the future, all while embracing the present moment. As travelers discover the simplicity and beauty of Monjas, they become part of a narrative that captures the essence of a destination where nature, culture, and community harmonize in perfect unity.

Pacaya Volcano: Journey into the Fiery Heart of Guatemala

In the rugged landscapes of Guatemala, a natural wonder stands as a testament to the Earth's fiery power and the beauty it creates. Pacaya Volcano, one of Central America's most active

volcanoes, captivates adventurers and nature enthusiasts with its towering presence, ever-changing landscapes, and the thrill of experiencing the forces that shape our planet. Rising from the heart of the country, Pacaya beckons travelers to embark on a journey that combines awe-inspiring geological marvels with the exhilaration of exploration. From its molten heart to the breathtaking vistas that surround it, Pacaya offers a unique and unforgettable encounter with the forces that have shaped Guatemala's dramatic landscapes.

Pacaya Volcano, part of the Pacific Ring of Fire, has a history dating back thousands of years. Its volcanic activity has left an indelible mark on the region's topography, creating a symphony of landscapes that range from lush forests to hardened lava fields. The volcano's silhouette rises dramatically from the landscape, its presence a reminder of the dynamic forces that continue to shape our planet.

Pacaya's designation as an active volcano adds to its allure, drawing adventurers seeking to witness the Earth's raw power in action. Its relatively frequent eruptions contribute to the ever-changing landscape, as new layers of lava reshape its contours. Travelers who venture to Pacaya have the chance to witness the volcano's activity up close, experiencing the rumbling, hissing, and mesmerizing glow of its molten core.

Exploring Pacaya is a journey into a world of geological marvels. As visitors trek along its trails, they traverse ancient lava fields that showcase the aftermath of past eruptions. The rugged terrain, sculpted by the flow of molten rock, is a testament to the transformative force of nature. The sight of solidified lava formations and the heat radiating from the Earth's core offer a visceral reminder of the planet's geological activity.

One of the highlights of a visit to Pacaya is the opportunity to hike to its summit. The hike, while demanding, rewards adventurers with panoramic views that stretch across the horizon. As travelers ascend, they may witness the volcanic landscape shift before their eyes, revealing the intricate patterns left by the flow of lava. Upon reaching the summit, the sight of the smoking crater and the breathtaking vistas of surrounding valleys and peaks are a reward that transcends the physical exertion.

A unique and thrilling experience awaits those who reach the summit of Pacaya: the chance to roast marshmallows over the volcano's warm, molten lava. Guides often carry sticks and marshmallows for visitors to enjoy this unusual treat. It's a moment that captures the juxtaposition of nature's power and the simple joys that travel offers.

Pacaya's landscapes are a palette of colors that change with the shifting light. From the vibrant green of the surrounding vegetation to the dark hues of the lava rocks, the volcano creates a mesmerizing contrast. As the sun rises or sets, the interplay of light and shadow transforms the terrain, painting a vivid and ever-changing picture that captivates the eye and the soul.

The surrounding communities bear witness to Pacaya's impact on their lives. The fertile soils nurtured by volcanic activity have allowed agricultural traditions to flourish, and the nearby towns and villages reflect the strength and resilience of those who call this region home. Interacting with locals offers travelers a glimpse into the balance between the power of nature and the tenacity of human spirit.

Pacaya is not only a geological wonder but also a living classroom for those who seek to understand the Earth's processes. Researchers and students alike find inspiration in its ever-changing landscapes and the scientific insights it offers. The volcano's activity provides an opportunity to study the dynamic forces that shape our world and offers a valuable window into the Earth's inner workings.

As visitors engage with the volcano's landscapes, they are reminded of the importance of environmental consciousness and responsible tourism. Pacaya's beauty is a result of the delicate balance between nature's power and human stewardship. Supporting conservation efforts and practicing responsible hiking and exploration allows travelers to enjoy the volcano's majesty while ensuring its preservation for future generations.

Journeying to Pacaya Volcano is an unforgettable encounter with the Earth's elemental forces. It's a voyage that evokes a sense of wonder, humility, and appreciation for the planet's incredible diversity. As travelers stand in awe before the volcano's majesty, witness its rumbling activity, and traverse its ancient lava fields, they become part of a narrative that spans millennia—a narrative that celebrates the beauty of our world's geological wonders and invites us to embrace the awe-inspiring power of nature.

Acatenango Volcano: A Majestic Ascent to Guatemala's Summit

In the heart of Guatemala's volcanic landscape, Acatenango Volcano rises as a towering sentinel that beckons adventurers to undertake a journey of unparalleled beauty and challenge. As one of the country's most iconic peaks, Acatenango offers intrepid explorers an opportunity to ascend into the heavens, witness the raw power of volcanic activity, and stand in awe of the panoramic vistas that stretch across the horizon. From its foothills to its summit, Acatenango provides a captivating blend of natural wonder, physical endurance, and the thrill of conquering new heights. This majestic volcano stands as a testament to the Earth's forces and the spirit of human exploration that knows no bounds.

Acatenango Volcano is part of the dramatic volcanic chain that defines Guatemala's topography. Its towering presence, reaching an elevation of over 13,000 feet, dominates the surrounding landscape and commands attention from miles away. The volcano's symmetrical cone and rugged contours create a sense of awe and anticipation for those who embark on the ascent.

Acatenango's proximity to the active Fuego Volcano adds to its allure. The two volcanoes are often referred to as the "Twin Volcanoes," with Acatenango providing an ideal vantage point to witness the fiery eruptions and molten lava flows of its more active counterpart. The relationship between these volcanoes is a reminder of the dynamic forces that have shaped the region's geological history.

Ascending Acatenango is a test of physical endurance and mental fortitude. The trek to the summit is a challenging endeavor that requires determination, stamina, and a willingness to overcome obstacles. Hikers traverse steep trails, navigate rugged terrain, and adjust to changing weather conditions as they ascend toward the peak. The journey demands commitment and offers rewards that are as immense as the challenges themselves.

Acatenango's ascent is often undertaken in stages, with hikers spending a night at one of the mountain's high-altitude campsites before making the final push to the summit. These campsites, nestled amidst the volcanic landscapes, offer a unique opportunity to experience the beauty of the night sky at high elevation. As the sun sets and darkness envelops the surroundings, the stars emerge in a dazzling display that ignites the imagination and connects hikers to the cosmos.

The pinnacle of the Acatenango experience is the sunrise from the summit. As hikers make the final ascent in the early morning hours, anticipation builds for the breathtaking reward that awaits. The moment the first rays of sunlight break over the horizon, casting an ethereal glow across the landscape, is an unforgettable sight that symbolizes triumph, beauty, and the indomitable spirit of exploration.

One of the most remarkable aspects of the Acatenango trek is the proximity to Fuego's volcanic activity. From the summit of Acatenango, travelers have the unique vantage point of witnessing Fuego's eruptions up close. The sight of molten lava spewing from the crater, accompanied by billowing ash and smoke, is a humbling reminder of the Earth's ongoing processes and the delicate balance between destruction and creation.

The reward for reaching Acatenango's summit is a panorama that defies description. The vistas stretch across the Guatemalan highlands, revealing a patchwork of landscapes that include fertile valleys, distant peaks, and the tranquil beauty of Lake Atitlán. The view is a testament to the Earth's artistry and the magic of exploration that unveils hidden treasures.

The Acatenango trek offers more than physical challenges—it provides a lesson in perspective. As hikers navigate the difficult terrain and overcome obstacles, they gain a deeper appreciation

for the power of determination, the beauty of the natural world, and the significance of embracing challenges. The journey becomes a metaphor for life's peaks and valleys, reminding travelers that growth and discovery often occur outside of comfort zones.

While ascending Acatenango, travelers have the opportunity to engage with the principles of conservation and preservation. The volcano's ecosystems are fragile, and responsible hiking practices are crucial to minimize the impact on the environment. By adhering to sustainable practices, travelers ensure that future generations can also experience the beauty and majesty of Acatenango.

Conquering Acatenango is more than a physical achievement—it's a triumph of the human spirit. It's a testament to the power of determination, the allure of exploration, and the fulfillment that comes from reaching new heights. Standing on the summit, with the vastness of the landscape before them, hikers are reminded that the world is full of wonders waiting to be discovered.

Embarking on an expedition to Acatenango Volcano is an unforgettable journey into the heart of Guatemala's natural wonders. It's a voyage that evokes a sense of awe, ignites the spirit of adventure, and connects travelers to the Earth's elemental forces. As hikers ascend its trails, witness its volcanic activity, and stand in awe of its panoramic views, they become part of a narrative that spans millennia—a narrative that celebrates the thrill of exploration and invites us to embrace the boundless beauty of our planet.

Chiquimula: Exploring the Heart of Eastern Guatemala

Nestled in the eastern region of Guatemala, Chiquimula emerges as a destination that offers a rich tapestry of culture, history, and natural beauty. With its vibrant markets, historic sites, and picturesque landscapes, Chiquimula beckons travelers to embark on a journey that unveils the stories of its past, celebrates its present, and showcases the diverse landscapes that define its identity. From its colonial heritage to its bustling markets, Chiquimula provides an authentic experience that captures the essence of Guatemala's cultural richness and the enduring spirit of its people.

Chiquimula's landscapes are a testament to the region's diversity. The town is surrounded by rolling hills, fertile valleys, and the majestic Sierra de las Minas mountain range. This varied topography creates a canvas of natural beauty that captivates the eye and offers travelers a range of experiences, from exploring arid plains to venturing into lush highlands.

The town's colonial heritage is reflected in the historic church of San Juan Ermita. This colonial-era gem stands as a testament to the architectural legacy left by the Spanish colonizers. The church's intricate façade and ornate details provide a glimpse into the past and the fusion of indigenous and European influences that shaped Chiquimula's history.

Chiquimula's markets are vibrant hubs of activity that offer a glimpse into the heart of local life. The Mercado Central, in particular, is a sensory delight where the aromas of fresh produce mingle with the colors of textiles, handicrafts, and local delicacies. Exploring these markets allows travelers to engage with locals, experience the rhythm of daily life, and discover the region's cultural treasures.

Chiquimula's religious traditions are celebrated through a calendar of festivals and events that showcase the town's spiritual heritage. From solemn processions to lively fiestas, these gatherings offer visitors a chance to witness the convergence of faith, culture, and community bonds. Participating in these celebrations provides an immersive experience of Chiquimula's cultural richness.

The Sierra de las Minas mountain range, which borders Chiquimula, is a natural sanctuary that offers opportunities for outdoor exploration and adventure. The cloud forests, diverse wildlife, and crystalline rivers of this protected area provide a haven for eco-tourism and conservation. Hiking through its trails allows travelers to immerse themselves in the beauty of Guatemala's natural world.

Chiquimula's culinary scene reflects its cultural diversity and agricultural abundance. Local dishes showcase the flavors of the region, often incorporating fresh produce and traditional ingredients. Exploring the town's eateries and engaging in culinary experiences offers visitors a chance to savor the authentic flavors that define Chiquimula's gastronomic identity.

Artisans in Chiquimula continue to uphold traditional craftsmanship, creating textiles, pottery, and other handicrafts that reflect the town's cultural heritage. Visitors can explore workshops, interact with artisans, and gain a deeper appreciation for the creativity and skill that define Chiquimula's artistic landscape.

Chiquimula invites travelers to embrace community connection and unity, fostering interactions with locals that transcend language barriers and cultural differences. Engaging with the town's inhabitants offers a firsthand experience of the warmth, hospitality, and strong sense of belonging that define the region.

Chiquimula's commitment to conservation is evident in its efforts to protect its natural and cultural heritage. The region's natural reserves and protected areas provide habitats for diverse flora and fauna, allowing travelers to experience the beauty of the environment while contributing to its preservation.

Chiquimula is a living tapestry that weaves together the threads of its past and present. Its colonial landmarks coexist with bustling markets, and its traditions are integral to daily life. As travelers traverse its landscapes, engage with its communities, and participate in its cultural events, they become part of Chiquimula's ongoing narrative—a narrative that celebrates heritage, embraces diversity, and invites visitors to experience the authenticity that defines this corner of Guatemala.

Exploring Chiquimula is an authentic encounter that reveals the layers of history, celebrates the spirit of community, and showcases the landscapes that envelop the town. It's a journey that pays homage to the legacies of the past and the aspirations of the future, all while immersing travelers in the vibrant tapestry of the present. As visitors connect with Chiquimula's culture, engage with its people, and appreciate its natural wonders, they become part of a narrative that captures the heart and soul of Guatemala's diverse and captivating essence.

El Mirador: Unveiling the Ancient Secrets of Guatemala's Lost City

In the heart of the Guatemalan jungle, a hidden treasure lies concealed by the lush foliage and towering trees. El Mirador, often referred to as "The Cradle of Maya Civilization," emerges as a captivating archaeological site that offers a window into the ancient past of the Maya people. Nestled within the Petén Basin, El Mirador beckons adventurers and history enthusiasts to embark on a journey that transcends time, unveiling the mysteries of a once-thriving civilization. From its towering pyramids to its intricate stelae, El Mirador invites travelers to immerse themselves in the rich history, cultural heritage, and architectural marvels that define this ancient city.

El Mirador's significance lies not only in its historical importance but also in its remote location amidst the dense rainforests of the Petén region. This archaeological gem has managed to preserve its secrets for centuries, hidden beneath layers of vegetation that protected the structures from the passage of time. As travelers venture into this jungle sanctuary, they step back in time and embark on an extraordinary archaeological expedition.

At the heart of El Mirador stands La Danta, a colossal pyramid that ranks among the largest structures of its kind in the world. The sheer size and scale of La Danta are a testament to the engineering prowess and organizational capabilities of the ancient Maya civilization. Climbing to the top of La Danta offers a panoramic view of the surrounding jungle, as well as a tangible connection to the past.

El Mirador's layout and urban planning reveal the sophistication of Maya society. The city was intricately designed, with ceremonial plazas, palaces, ball courts, and intricate networks of causeways that connected various structures. Exploring the pathways and plazas of El Mirador offers insights into the organization and functionality of the ancient city, providing a glimpse into the daily lives of its inhabitants.

The stelae (stone monuments) of El Mirador serve as historical records etched in stone. These intricately carved sculptures depict scenes of rulers, rituals, and cosmological beliefs of the Maya civilization. The stelae are a testament to the Maya's artistic skill and the importance of recording their history for future generations.

El Mirador's excavation and preservation efforts are ongoing, as archaeologists work tirelessly to uncover its hidden treasures and decipher the secrets it holds. The site's remote location presents challenges, but the rewards are immeasurable—a deeper understanding of Maya culture, history, and the evolution of their civilization. Travelers who visit El Mirador contribute to its preservation and support the research that sheds light on the past.

Exploring El Mirador is an opportunity to connect with the ancients, to stand in awe before their architectural achievements, and to imagine the bustling city that once thrived in the heart of the jungle. The echoes of ceremonies, conversations, and daily life resonate through the ruins, inviting visitors to be part of an experience that transcends the boundaries of time.

El Mirador serves as a time capsule that offers insights into Maya society, politics, religion, and daily life. As travelers wander through its plazas and stand before its monuments, they gain a deeper appreciation for the intricate belief systems, cultural practices, and technological innovations that defined the Maya civilization.

Visiting El Mirador comes with a responsibility to respect and preserve the site for future generations. Travelers are urged to adhere to responsible tourism practices, including following designated trails, avoiding touching or climbing on structures, and minimizing their impact on the environment. By treading lightly, visitors contribute to the preservation of El Mirador's historical and natural legacy.

Exploring El Mirador is more than a physical journey—it's a voyage into the unknown, a quest to uncover the stories that have shaped human history. As travelers walk in the footsteps of the Maya, they become part of a narrative that spans millennia—a narrative of discovery, wonder, and the enduring quest for knowledge. El Mirador beckons the curious, the adventurous, and the seekers of ancient truths to embark on a journey that transcends the ordinary and reveals the extraordinary.

Iximché: A Glimpse into Guatemala's Indigenous Past

Nestled within the highlands of Guatemala, the ancient ruins of Iximché stand as a testament to the rich history and cultural heritage of the Maya civilization. With its ceremonial plazas, intricate temples, and vibrant history, Iximché offers travelers a unique opportunity to step back in time and explore the remnants of a once-thriving indigenous capital. As the former capital of the Kaqchikel Maya kingdom, Iximché invites visitors to immerse themselves in the stories of the past, engage with the traditions of the present, and connect with the enduring spirit of Guatemala's indigenous communities.

Iximché, meaning "tree of maize" in the Kaqchikel language, stands as a window to the past, allowing us to glimpse the complex societies that flourished in the region long before the arrival of European colonizers. The ruins provide a tangible connection to the indigenous civilizations that shaped the landscape, engaged in trade, and practiced their religious rituals amidst the natural beauty of the Guatemalan highlands.

The layout of Iximché reflects its ceremonial significance in the Maya world. The site is adorned with plazas, altars, ball courts, and pyramidal structures that served as religious and administrative centers. These architectural elements offer insights into the spiritual practices, social organization, and cultural values of the indigenous communities that once inhabited the area.

Iximché's historical significance is tied to its role as the capital of the Kaqchikel Maya kingdom during the Late Postclassic period. The site was chosen for its strategic location and proximity to fertile lands, which facilitated agricultural production and trade. The remains of temples, palace structures, and council chambers stand as testament to the political and cultural importance of Iximché in the region.

Iximché's significance extends beyond its historical and architectural value—it remains a living testament to the spiritual heritage of the Maya people. The site was used for important religious ceremonies, including offerings and rituals to honor deities and ancestors. The energy of these rituals is still palpable in the air, creating an atmosphere that resonates with the ancient beliefs of the Maya.

Exploring Iximché is a multi-sensory experience that engages sight, sound, and imagination. As visitors walk through the plazas, ascend the pyramids, and explore the remnants of structures, they are transported to a different era. The panoramic views from the hilltops offer vistas of the surrounding landscapes, creating a sense of connection to the natural world that was integral to the Maya way of life.

Iximché continues to yield archaeological discoveries that shed light on the history of the Maya civilization. Excavations have unearthed pottery, sculptures, and other artifacts that provide insights into the daily lives, artistic expressions, and technological advancements of the indigenous communities. These discoveries contribute to a deeper understanding of the cultural mosaic that defined the region.

Iximché's cultural legacy extends to the present day, as the site remains a sacred place for contemporary indigenous communities. Rituals, ceremonies, and cultural events continue to be held at the ruins, reflecting the enduring connection between the past and the present. Visitors who witness these events gain a deeper appreciation for the resilience of indigenous traditions.

Iximché's preservation and conservation efforts are essential to ensuring that its historical and cultural legacy is passed on to future generations. The delicate balance between maintaining the site's authenticity and protecting it from the impacts of tourism and the environment requires a collective commitment to responsible tourism practices.

Exploring Iximché is more than a visit to archaeological ruins—it's a journey through time that bridges the gap between ancient civilizations and contemporary indigenous communities. As visitors walk in the footsteps of the Maya, they become part of a narrative that celebrates heritage, embraces diversity, and honors the resilience of the human spirit.

Iximché offers travelers the opportunity to engage in cultural exchange and appreciation. Interacting with local communities, learning about their traditions, and participating in ceremonies fosters a deeper understanding of indigenous cultures and challenges preconceived notions. This exchange enriches the travel experience and broadens perspectives.

Visiting Iximché is an immersive encounter that transcends the boundaries of time and space. It's an opportunity to stand amidst the ruins that once witnessed the rituals, celebrations, and stories of a vibrant civilization. As visitors explore the plazas, ascend the pyramids, and contemplate the history that echoes through the stones, they become part of Iximché's ongoing narrative—a narrative that celebrates the resilience of indigenous cultures, invites dialogue, and fosters a deeper appreciation for Guatemala's rich cultural tapestry.

Barrio de San Felipe: A Cultural Tapestry of Antigua Guatemala

Nestled within the charming streets of Antigua Guatemala, the Barrio de San Felipe emerges as a cultural gem that weaves together history, artistry, and vibrant community life. With its

cobblestone lanes, colonial architecture, and artistic flair, this neighborhood invites travelers to embark on a journey that celebrates the essence of Antigua's colonial past and the creative spirit of its present. From its historic landmarks to its bustling markets, Barrio de San Felipe provides an authentic experience that captures the heart and soul of this captivating corner of Guatemala.

Barrio de San Felipe's cobbled streets and well-preserved colonial architecture evoke the charm of Antigua's past. As visitors stroll through its narrow lanes, they are transported to an era when horse-drawn carriages echoed through the streets and the plazas were gathering places for the community. The neighborhood's historical significance is palpable in every step, offering a glimpse into the town's colonial heritage.

The architecture of Barrio de San Felipe reflects the rich history of Antigua Guatemala. Adorned with colorful facades, ornate ironwork, and intricate wooden doors, the buildings stand as testaments to the Spanish colonial influence that shaped the town's character. Landmarks such as the San Felipe Church and Convent add a spiritual dimension to the neighborhood, inviting contemplation and connection with the town's religious history.

Barrio de San Felipe is a haven for artistic expression, drawing both local and international creatives. The neighborhood is dotted with galleries, studios, and workshops where artists of various disciplines gather to create and share their work. The fusion of traditional techniques and contemporary concepts produces a vibrant artistic tapestry that enriches the cultural fabric of the community.

The neighborhood's plazas and open spaces serve as community gathering points, where residents and visitors alike come together to celebrate traditions and festivities. From religious processions to lively street festivals, Barrio de San Felipe pulsates with the rhythms of communal life. Participating in these events allows travelers to engage with locals and witness the deep sense of pride and unity that defines the neighborhood.

The Mercado de San Felipe is a sensory delight that captures the flavors and aromas of Guatemala. This bustling market showcases a colorful array of fresh produce, local ingredients, and traditional dishes. Exploring the market offers travelers an opportunity to taste the authentic flavors of Antigua, interact with vendors, and gain insights into the culinary traditions that define Guatemalan cuisine.

Barrio de San Felipe's commitment to preservation is evident in its efforts to maintain its colonial architecture and historical sites. The neighborhood's authenticity has been carefully preserved, allowing visitors to experience the ambiance of centuries past. Responsible tourism practices, such as respectful exploration and support for local artisans, contribute to the preservation of the neighborhood's cultural heritage.

Engaging with the residents of Barrio de San Felipe offers travelers a chance to connect on a personal level and gain insights into the daily lives and traditions of the community. Interacting with artisans, sharing stories with locals, and participating in neighborhood events fosters cultural exchange and creates meaningful connections that enrich the travel experience.

Barrio de San Felipe has evolved into a creative hub that nurtures artistic endeavors and fosters a sense of community among creatives. From traditional crafts to contemporary art forms, the neighborhood provides a platform for artists to showcase their talents and engage in dialogue with both local and global audiences.

Exploring Barrio de San Felipe is an immersion into an ongoing narrative that celebrates heritage, creativity, and human connection. The neighborhood's historic streets, artistic energy, and community bonds create an atmosphere of authenticity that resonates with travelers. As visitors traverse its lanes, engage with its residents, and appreciate its artistic expressions, they become part of a story that captures the heart of Antigua's past and the vitality of its present.

Barrio de San Felipe is more than a neighborhood—it's a living tapestry that embodies the soul of Antigua Guatemala. It's a place where history and artistry converge, where traditions are celebrated, and where the spirit of community thrives. As travelers explore its streets, engage with its people, and absorb its cultural vibrancy, they become part of a woven narrative that celebrates the past, embraces the present, and invites them to share in the collective story of this captivating corner of Guatemala.

Section 5: Cuisine

Savoring the Flavors of Guatemala: Best Cuisine and Street Food Delights

Guatemala's culinary scene is a sensory adventure that reflects the country's diverse cultural heritage, rich history, and vibrant flavors. From traditional dishes passed down through generations to the lively street food scene that thrives in local markets and bustling corners,

Guatemala's cuisine offers a tantalizing journey for food enthusiasts. Here are some of the best dishes and street food delights to savor in Guatemala:

1. Pepián: A Hearty Stew of Mayan Origins

Pepián is a rich and flavorful stew that traces its roots to ancient Mayan cuisine. This dish combines meats (often chicken or beef), vegetables, and a blend of spices to create a robust and aromatic flavor profile. The use of ingredients like pumpkin seeds and dried chilies gives Pepián its distinctive taste. It's often served with rice and tortillas, making it a complete and satisfying meal.

2. Kak'ik: A Traditional Mayan Turkey Soup

Kak'ik is a traditional Mayan soup that features turkey as its star ingredient. Prepared with a variety of aromatic herbs and spices, Kak'ik offers a complex and earthy flavor profile. The broth is rich and hearty, often accompanied by ingredients like tamalitos (small tamales) and potatoes. This dish is not only a culinary delight but also a cultural symbol with deep historical significance.

3. Tamales: Wrapped Parcels of Flavor

Tamales hold a special place in Guatemalan cuisine and culture. These wrapped parcels of masa (corn dough) are filled with a variety of ingredients such as meats, vegetables, and sauces. They

are wrapped in plantain leaves and steamed to perfection. Tamales are often enjoyed during special occasions and celebrations, making them a beloved culinary tradition.

4. Chiles Rellenos: A Spicy Delight

Chiles rellenos are a mouthwatering dish that showcases the creativity of Guatemalan cooks. This dish consists of large chili peppers stuffed with a mixture of minced meat, vegetables, and seasonings. The peppers are then coated in a fluffy egg batter and fried until golden. The result is a harmonious blend of flavors and textures, often served with a tomato sauce.

5. Guatemalan Street Food: A Burst of Flavors

Guatemala's street food scene is a vibrant and dynamic part of its culinary landscape. Street vendors offer an array of delights that cater to both locals and curious travelers. Some street food favorites include:

- Chuchitos: Similar to tamales, these smaller versions are often filled with meats, cheese, or beans and served with a side of tomato salsa.

- Elote Loco: A popular street snack, elote loco consists of grilled corn on the cob smothered in mayonnaise, cheese, chili powder, and other toppings.

- Rellenitos: Sweet and savory collide in rellenitos, which are fried plantain dough filled with sweet black bean paste.

- Tostadas: Crispy tortillas topped with a variety of ingredients such as beans, cheese, avocado, and meats.

Pepián: A Hearty Stew of Mayan Origins

Guatemala's culinary landscape is a tapestry of flavors that reflects the country's rich cultural heritage, ancient traditions, and vibrant history. At the heart of this culinary journey lies a dish that embodies the essence of Guatemalan cuisine: Pepián. This hearty stew, with its intricate blend of ingredients and robust flavors, is more than just a meal—it's a culinary masterpiece that carries the legacy of Mayan origins and the creative spirit of Guatemala's people.

To truly appreciate the significance of Pepián, we must travel back in time to the ancient Mayan civilization that laid the foundation for Guatemalan culture. The Mayans, known for their sophisticated agricultural practices and culinary prowess, cultivated a diverse array of ingredients that would eventually become integral to dishes like Pepián. Maize, beans, squash, chilies, and cocoa were staples of their diet, forming the basis of many Mayan meals.

Pepián's origins can be traced to the intersection of Mayan culinary traditions and Spanish influences. The dish evolved during the colonial era, as the Spanish introduced new ingredients and cooking techniques to the indigenous populations. The result was a harmonious fusion of indigenous ingredients and Spanish flavors—a blend that continues to define Pepián.

At its core, Pepián is a meat stew that showcases the artistry of Guatemalan cooks. The dish's complexity lies in its combination of textures and flavors, achieved through a meticulous layering of ingredients. The traditional base of Pepián includes roasted tomatoes, tomatillos, onions, garlic, and spices. This flavorful foundation sets the stage for the diverse range of ingredients that follow.

The key to Pepián's richness is the addition of toasted and ground seeds, whichh vary based on regional and personal preferences. Pumpkin seeds (pepitas) and sesame seeds are commonly used, contributing a nutty undertone and a velvety texture to the stew. These seeds are painstakingly toasted and ground to create a paste known as "recado," which is the heart of Pepián's flavor profile.

Pepián traditionally features meat as its protein source, with chicken, beef, or pork being common choices. The meat is simmered in the recado along with vegetables such as potatoes, carrots, and green beans. This combination of ingredients creates a harmonious balance between the richness of the recado and the hearty, satisfying elements of the stew.

The beauty of Pepián lies in its ability to capture a symphony of flavors within a single dish. The recado, enriched with ground seeds and spices, infuses the meat and vegetables with a depth of flavor that tantalizes the palate. The stew's profile is a harmonious blend of earthy, nutty, and savory notes, punctuated by the gentle heat of chilies. The result is a taste that is at once comforting and complex, a testament to the culinary ingenuity of Guatemalan cooks.

Pepián is more than just a meal—it's a cultural touchstone that connects Guatemalans to their Mayan heritage and their shared history. The dish is often served during celebrations, family gatherings, and special occasions, making it a symbol of togetherness and shared joy. As families gather around the table to enjoy Pepián, they also honor the traditions that have been passed down through generations.

One of the fascinating aspects of Pepián is its regional diversity. Different regions of Guatemala have their own interpretations of the dish, incorporating local ingredients and culinary traditions. For example, in the city of Antigua, Pepián is often served with rice, while in other

regions, it might be accompanied by tortillas or tamalitos. This regional diversity adds depth to the narrative of Pepián and highlights the unique characteristics of each area.

Pepián's legacy extends beyond the confines of a single dish—it is a reflection of the resilience and creativity of the Guatemalan people. The stew's journey from ancient Mayan traditions to modern-day dining tables tells a story of cultural exchange, adaptation, and preservation. As travelers savor Pepián's rich flavors, they become part of this narrative, celebrating the heritage that has shaped Guatemala's culinary identity.

Indulging in a bowl of Pepián is more than just a gustatory experience—it's an immersion into the heart and soul of Guatemala. The dish encapsulates the country's history, its indigenous roots, and the artistry of its culinary traditions. As the aroma of toasted seeds and spices fills the air and the first spoonful is savored, travelers embark on a sensory journey that transcends time and place. Pepián invites us to appreciate the beauty of tradition, the power of flavor, and the universal language of food that unites us all.

Kak'ik: A Journey into the Essence of Mayan Cuisine

In the heart of Guatemala, a traditional Mayan soup known as Kak'ik stands as a culinary emblem of heritage, community, and reverence. This complex and flavorful dish captures the essence of Mayan cuisine, offering a glimpse into the traditions and rituals that have shaped Guatemala's cultural tapestry. Kak'ik is more than just a soup—it's a sensory journey that invites us to explore the ancient roots, spiritual significance, and culinary artistry that define this unique dish.

Kak'ik traces its origins back to the ancient Mayan civilization, a period characterized by sophisticated agricultural practices and a deep connection to the land. The Mayans revered turkey as a sacred bird, symbolizing abundance and spiritual significance. Kak'ik, which features turkey as its central ingredient, pays homage to this reverence for nature and spirituality that is deeply ingrained in Mayan culture.

Kak'ik is a culinary masterpiece that embodies the Mayan principle of balance—balancing flavors, textures, and ingredients to create a harmonious whole. The soup is characterized by its complexity, with layers of flavors that dance on the palate. The foundation of Kak'ik is the rich, spiced broth infused with aromatic herbs and ingredients.

At the heart of Kak'ik's flavor profile is "recado," a paste made from roasted and ground spices, seeds, and herbs. This recado serves as the base for the soup, infusing it with a deep and robust taste. The recado's composition may vary, but it often includes ingredients like allspice, achiote

(annatto), oregano, and black pepper. The process of preparing the recado is a labor of love, involving toasting and grinding the spices to perfection.

Turkey is the star of Kak'ik, and its presence in the soup carries both culinary and spiritual significance. The tender turkey meat, cooked to perfection, imparts a rich and meaty flavor to the broth. In Mayan culture, the turkey is considered a symbol of fertility and abundance, and its inclusion in Kak'ik is a nod to the Mayans' deep connection to nature and their respect for the cycle of life.

Kak'ik's aromatic profile is a sensory delight that transports us to the heart of Mayan landscapes. Ingredients like cilantro, mint, and hierba mora (black nightshade) infuse the soup with fresh, herbal notes. These aromatics not only enhance the flavor but also contribute to the therapeutic and medicinal qualities of the dish.

Beyond its culinary allure, Kak'ik carries spiritual significance in Mayan culture. The dish is often prepared for special occasions, ceremonies, and rituals, serving as a symbol of community and connection. In some Mayan communities, Kak'ik is associated with the Day of the Dead celebrations, where families gather to honor their ancestors and share a meal that bridges the earthly and spiritual realms.

The preparation of Kak'ik is a communal effort that brings families and communities together. From sourcing the ingredients to painstakingly crafting the recado, each step of the process is infused with tradition and shared labor. The act of preparing Kak'ik is a reminder of the importance of unity, cooperation, and the bonds that connect generations.

Kak'ik's nutritional value extends beyond its flavorful taste. The soup is made from locally sourced ingredients, emphasizing the importance of utilizing resources that the land provides. With its blend of turkey, vegetables, herbs, and spices, Kak'ik offers a balanced and nourishing meal that reflects the Mayans' deep understanding of food as medicine.

While Kak'ik's origins lie in Mayan antiquity, the dish remains an integral part of Guatemala's culinary fabric. In both rural kitchens and urban restaurants, Kak'ik continues to be prepared and enjoyed. Its enduring presence is a testament to the resilience of Mayan traditions and the adaptability of Guatemalan cuisine.

For those fortunate enough to savor a bowl of Kak'ik, the experience is akin to embarking on a culinary pilgrimage. The first spoonful introduces a symphony of flavors—warm and inviting, complex yet comforting. With each taste, we connect not only with the dish's intricate flavors but also with the Mayans' reverence for nature, their rituals, and their shared history.

Kak'ik transcends the boundaries of a simple dish—it is a symbol of identity, heritage, and the interconnectedness of past and present. As we delve into the depths of this Mayan

masterpiece, we immerse ourselves in the stories of an ancient culture, the wisdom of the land, and the culinary traditions that have nurtured communities for generations.

Kak'ik weaves together the threads of Guatemala's Mayan heritage, its cultural rituals, and its culinary artistry into a rich and flavorful tapestry. As we sip from a bowl of this nourishing soup, we are invited to savor not only the taste but also the history, spirituality, and collective memory that have shaped Kak'ik into the cherished dish it is today.

Tamales: Unwrapping the Essence of Guatemala's Culinary Heritage

In the heart of Guatemala's vibrant culinary landscape lies a cherished tradition that has transcended centuries and woven itself into the fabric of daily life: tamales. These iconic wrapped parcels of flavor serve as more than just a meal—they are a testament to Guatemala's rich cultural heritage, a symbol of community, and a culinary art form that bridges the past with the present. From bustling markets to family gatherings, tamales hold a special place in the hearts and palates of Guatemalans, inviting us to unwrap the layers of history, creativity, and taste that define this beloved dish.

Tamales have an ancient history that predates the Spanish colonial era, dating back to the indigenous civilizations that flourished in Mesoamerica. The Mayans and Aztecs, known for their sophisticated agricultural practices, revered maize (corn) as a sacred staple. The humble maize formed the foundation of tamales, serving as both sustenance and ritual offerings in ancient cultures.

At its essence, a tamale is a harmonious blend of masa (corn dough), filling, and wrapping. The process of crafting tamales involves a series of intricate steps, each contributing to the final masterpiece. The masa is prepared by grinding soaked corn kernels into a dough, which is then seasoned with ingredients like lard, broth, and spices. This base forms the canvas upon which a myriad of flavors and textures are layered.

Tamales are a canvas for culinary creativity, with fillings that vary based on region, tradition, and personal preference. From savory to sweet, the possibilities are as diverse as the landscapes that define Guatemala. Common fillings include shredded meats (chicken, pork, or beef), vegetables, cheese, beans, and even chocolate for dessert tamales. The filling is carefully placed atop the masa, creating a delicate balance of taste and texture.

Wrapping tamales is a skill that reflects generations of knowledge and hands-on experience. Banana leaves or corn husks serve as the vessel, imparting a subtle aroma and contributing to the tamale's distinctive appearance. The masa and filling are carefully encased within the leaf or husk, resulting in a neatly folded parcel that is tied with thin strips of leaves. This process is a labor of love, one that embodies the care and attention that goes into creating tamales.

Tamales hold deep cultural significance in Guatemala, serving as an emblem of tradition, family, and celebration. They are often prepared for special occasions, holidays, and religious ceremonies. In Guatemala's diverse cultural landscape, tamales are associated with specific celebrations such as Christmas, New Year's, and Dia de Todos los Santos (All Saints' Day). The act of making tamales is a communal affair, bringing families and communities together to share stories, laughter, and generations-old techniques.

For many Guatemalans, tamales are not only a cherished dish but also a reflection of cultural identity. They provide a tangible link to ancestral traditions and a way of passing down heritage to younger generations. The aroma of tamales steaming in the kitchen, the sound of laughter during the preparation, and the taste of each carefully crafted bite are all integral to the narrative of Guatemalan families and their culinary journey.

Guatemala's regional diversity is mirrored in its tamale variations. Each region offers its own unique interpretation, reflecting local ingredients, culinary practices, and cultural influences. From the hearty tamales colorados of Guatemala City to the sweet kak'ik tamales of the Ixil region, these variations serve as a testament to the country's gastronomic diversity.

Tamales are not confined to the kitchen—Guatemala's vibrant street food scene also features these wrapped delights. Street vendors set up stalls in bustling markets and street corners, offering a convenient and delicious option for those on the go. These tamales, often served with a side of spicy tomato sauce, provide a taste of authenticity for both locals and curious travelers.

As Guatemala's culinary gem, tamales go beyond geographical borders and linguistic barriers. They embody the universal language of food—a language that transcends cultures and unites people in the act of sharing a meal. Travelers who indulge in a tamale find themselves partaking in a time-honored tradition that links them to generations of cooks, artisans, and families who have contributed to this culinary legacy.

Savoring a tamale is more than just experiencing a delicious meal—it's immersing oneself in the essence of Guatemala. It's a taste of history, a celebration of tradition, and a reflection of the country's cultural richness. The layers of masa, filling, and wrapping tell a story that stretches back centuries, connecting modern-day Guatemalans to their roots.

In each tamale, there's a legacy—a legacy of flavor, of creativity, and of love. From the hands that craft them to the hearts that savor them, tamales are a testament to the resilience of

Guatemalan culture and the enduring power of culinary traditions. As we unwrap the layers of a tamale, we uncover not just the ingredients within but the stories, memories, and connections that make it a cherished emblem of Guatemala's culinary heritage.

Chiles Rellenos: A Spicy Delight that Ignites the Palate

In the heart of Guatemala's vibrant culinary scene, there exists a dish that combines the artistry of cooking with the allure of spice: Chiles Rellenos. This savory masterpiece, a culinary delight of stuffed chili peppers, is a celebration of flavors, textures, and the skilled hands that bring it to life. From its humble beginnings to its status as a beloved comfort food, Chiles Rellenos holds a special place in Guatemalan cuisine—a dish that exemplifies the country's passion for culinary creativity and its rich cultural tapestry.

The origins of Chiles Rellenos can be traced back to Mexico, where the dish first emerged as a result of the fusion between Spanish and indigenous culinary traditions. As Spanish conquistadors introduced new ingredients to the New World, they encountered indigenous peppers and cooking techniques. The marriage of these elements gave birth to Chiles Rellenos—a dish that soon found its way into the hearts and kitchens of people across Latin America, including Guatemala.

At its core, Chiles Rellenos is a culinary work of art that centers around the concept of stuffing peppers with a flavorful mixture. The choice of peppers varies, with poblano peppers being a popular option due to their size and mild heat. The peppers are carefully roasted or charred to impart a smoky flavor, and then the inner seeds and membranes are removed, leaving a hollow vessel ready to be filled.

The heart of Chiles Rellenos lies in the filling—a creative amalgamation of ingredients that elevate the dish from simple to sensational. Traditional fillings often include a mixture of minced meats, vegetables, and cheese. The interplay of textures, from the tender meat to the melting cheese, creates a harmonious balance that entices the palate. Additional ingredients such as herbs, spices, and even fruits can be incorporated to enhance the depth of flavor.

Once the peppers are filled to perfection, they are delicately coated in an egg batter that adds a layer of richness and texture. The batter not only provides a protective shield for the filling but also transforms the peppers into a golden and crispy delight upon frying. The result is a seamless marriage of flavors—a marriage that delights the senses with each bite.

The process of frying the stuffed peppers is a crucial step that transforms Chiles Rellenos into a culinary masterpiece. The peppers are carefully placed in hot oil, and the batter puffs up to create a crisp and airy exterior. The artistry lies in achieving the perfect balance between a crispy outer layer and a tender filling, which requires skill and precision.

Chiles Rellenos often come bathed in a luscious tomato sauce, the final touch that ties the dish together. The sauce adds a burst of acidity and tanginess that complements the richness of the filling and the crispiness of the exterior. Variations of the sauce can include ingredients such as tomatoes, onions, garlic, and a medley of spices, resulting in a flavor profile that is both comforting and invigorating.

Beyond its culinary appeal, Chiles Rellenos holds cultural significance that is deeply ingrained in Guatemalan traditions. The dish is often served during special occasions, celebrations, and family gatherings. It's a testament to the warmth of Guatemalan hospitality, inviting loved ones to gather around the table and share a meal that embodies comfort and connection.

Chiles Rellenos encapsulates the essence of Guatemalan flavors—a combination of spices, creativity, and a touch of heat that speaks to the country's love for bold tastes. With each bite, diners embark on a sensory journey that unearths the layers of smokiness, the explosion of flavors, and the hint of spice that dance on the palate.

For many Guatemalans, Chiles Rellenos are more than just a dish—they are a taste of home, a connection to childhood memories, and a link to generations past. The dish's presence at family gatherings and special events instills a sense of nostalgia, evoking moments of joy, laughter, and togetherness.

As Guatemala's culinary landscape evolves, Chiles Rellenos remains a timeless favorite that continues to capture the hearts of both locals and visitors. It's a dish that pays homage to the past while embracing the future, adapting to modern tastes and preferences while retaining its authentic essence.

Indulging in Chiles Rellenos is embarking on a culinary adventure that goes beyond the plate. It's an exploration of history, culture, and the passion that defines Guatemalan cuisine. With each bite, diners experience the harmony of textures, the burst of flavors, and the warmth of a dish that has stood the test of time.

In the world of Guatemalan cuisine, Chiles Rellenos shines as a culinary gem that ignites the senses. Its layers of flavor, creativity, and cultural significance make it a dish worth savoring— one that encapsulates the heart and soul of Guatemala's culinary heritage. As the aroma of frying peppers fills the air and the first taste awakens the palate, Chiles Rellenos invites us to partake in a gastronomic experience that celebrates the artistry of cooking and the joy of sharing.

Guatemalan Street Food: A Flavorful Adventure on Every Corner

Guatemala's bustling streets come alive with an array of street food stalls, where aromas mingle with the sounds of laughter and the sights of colorful ingredients. Street food is more than just a quick bite—it's a vibrant culinary culture that invites locals and visitors to explore the diverse flavors and rich heritage of the country. From savory snacks to sweet delights, Guatemalan street food offers a burst of flavors that tell stories of tradition, innovation, and a passion for good food.

Tacos: The Quintessential Street Food

Tacos reign as one of the most beloved street food items in Guatemala. These handheld delights feature soft corn tortillas filled with an assortment of ingredients that range from succulent meats like carne asada (grilled beef) and chorizo (sausage) to vegetarian options like grilled cactus and beans. Topped with fresh salsa, onions, and cilantro, each taco is a bite-sized explosion of flavor that captures the essence of Guatemalan street food.

Empanadas: Portable Pockets of Deliciousness

Empanadas, known as "pastelitos" in Guatemala, are another street food favorite. These golden pockets of dough are filled with a variety of ingredients such as ground meat, cheese, potatoes, or vegetables. Empanadas offer a satisfying blend of textures—the crispy crust gives way to a flavorful filling that delights the taste buds with its savory and hearty taste.

Tostadas: Layers of Crunch and Flavor

Tostadas are a staple of Guatemalan street food—a symphony of crunch and taste. These crispy tortillas are topped with an array of ingredients, creating a vibrant tapestry of flavors. From refried beans and shredded chicken to chopped lettuce, tomatoes, cheese, and a drizzle of hot sauce, tostadas showcase the art of layering ingredients to create a balanced and satisfying bite.

Elote Loco: Grilled Corn Magic

Elote Loco, which translates to "Crazy Corn," is a street food delight that captures the essence of Guatemalan street culture. A skewered cob of corn is grilled to perfection and then smothered in a medley of toppings—mayonnaise, crumbled cheese, chili powder, and lime juice. The combination of creamy, tangy, and spicy flavors creates a harmonious blend that transforms a simple cob of corn into a taste sensation.

Rellenitos: Sweet and Savory Indulgence

Rellenitos are a unique Guatemalan street food that brings together the flavors of sweet and savory. These fried delicacies feature a filling of mashed black beans sweetened with panela (unrefined cane sugar), wrapped in a layer of mashed plantains, and then fried to a golden crisp. The contrast between the sweet plantains and the savory bean filling makes for a memorable culinary experience.

Pupusas: A Taste of Tradition

While pupusas are more commonly associated with neighboring El Salvador, they have made their way into the hearts of Guatemalan street food enthusiasts. These thick, stuffed tortillas are filled with ingredients such as cheese, beans, or meats, and they're griddled to perfection. Served with curtido (a pickled cabbage slaw) and tomato sauce, pupusas offer a taste of traditional Central American flavors.

Chuchitos: Guatemala's Tamale Delights

Chuchitos are a smaller, handheld version of Guatemala's beloved tamales. These portable delights feature masa (corn dough) filled with ingredients like meat, cheese, or beans, wrapped in a corn husk, and then steamed. Chuchitos are often enjoyed with a side of salsa, adding a kick of heat to each flavorful bite.

Fresh Fruit Juices: Nature's Refreshment

Guatemala's tropical climate provides the perfect backdrop for refreshing fruit juices offered by street vendors. From watermelon and pineapple to mango and papaya, these natural juices are blended on the spot, creating a revitalizing treat that cools down even the warmest days. The burst of sweetness and the vibrant colors make each sip a delightful experience.

Bocadillos: Sweet Bites of Guilty Pleasure

Bocadillos, which translate to "little bites," are Guatemalan street food desserts that offer a dose of sugary indulgence. These small, sweet treats come in various forms, such as cocadas (coconut candies), nuegados (fried dough), and atolillo (cornstarch pudding). Bocadillos are a guilty pleasure that satisfies cravings for sweetness and offers a taste of traditional Guatemalan confections.

Chapines and Guatemalan Delights

Chapines are Guatemalan snacks that encapsulate the flavors of the country. These street food bites include a variety of offerings, from pepitorias (roasted pumpkin seeds) and chilacayotes (candied squash) to dulces de leche (caramel candies) and more. These small bites Provide a taste of local ingredients and culinary traditions that have been passed down through generations.

Exploring Guatemalan street food is a culinary adventure that takes you through the vibrant streets, bustling markets, and lively corners of the country. Each bite offers a snapshot of Guatemalan life—where food is more than sustenance; it's a way of connecting, sharing, and celebrating the diverse flavors that define Guatemala's rich culinary heritage. As you savor each morsel of street food, you immerse yourself in a tapestry of flavors that tell stories of tradition, innovation, and the ever-evolving passion for good food.

Tacos: The Quintessential Street Food that Unites Taste and Tradition

In the bustling streets of Guatemala, an irresistible aroma wafts through the air, drawing locals and visitors alike to a beloved culinary delight: tacos. These handheld treasures, with their harmonious blend of flavors, textures, and cultural significance, stand as more than just a meal. Tacos are a testament to Guatemala's rich culinary heritage, a reflection of its diverse influences, and a celebration of the art of street food. From the sizzle of the grill to the first satisfying bite, tacos embody the essence of Guatemalan street food culture.

Tacos trace their origins to Mexico, where they emerged as a simple yet ingenious way of enjoying flavorful ingredients. The word "taco" itself translates to "plug" or "wad," referring to the practice of using tortillas to scoop up fillings. As Mexican culinary traditions spread across

Central America, tacos found a warm welcome in Guatemala, adapting to local tastes and ingredients. Over time, they evolved into a cherished street food, bridging cultural gaps and unifying appetites.

At the heart of every taco lies the tortilla—a delicate, thin, round flatbread made from maize (corn). In Guatemala, maize is not just an ingredient; it's a cultural cornerstone deeply rooted in Mayan history. The tortilla serves as the canvas upon which the taco's flavors are painted. Hand-pressed and griddled to perfection, the tortilla's aroma and texture set the stage for the culinary symphony that follows.

What truly distinguishes tacos is the limitless array of fillings that cater to every palate. From succulent meats to vibrant vegetables, the options are as diverse as Guatemala's landscapes. Carne asada (grilled beef), pollo (chicken), cerdo (pork), and chorizo (sausage) are popular meat fillings, each marinated and grilled to perfection. For vegetarians, grilled cactus, beans, cheese, and sautéed mushrooms provide delicious alternatives.

No taco experience is complete without the salsas and condiments that add a burst of flavor and heat. Salsa roja (red salsa) and salsa verde (green salsa) are staples, each crafted from a medley of ingredients like tomatoes, onions, chili peppers, and cilantro. The salsas infuse each bite with a zesty kick, enhancing the overall flavor profile and showcasing the marriage of taste and tradition.

Tacos master the art of texture play, offering a symphony of sensations in every bite. The tender meat contrasts with the crunch of fresh vegetables. Creamy guacamole and crema balance the heat of the salsa. And the tortilla itself offers a delicate layer that holds the ensemble together. Each element is carefully orchestrated to create a harmonious experience that appeals to the senses.

The assembly of a taco is a skillful process that requires attention to detail and a dash of creativity. The tortilla is placed on the grill, warmed to perfection, and then filled with the chosen ingredients. The toppings—onions, cilantro, and lime—add the finishing touches that elevate the taco from a mere dish to a work of art. The final product is a testament to the dedication of the street food vendors who craft each taco with care.

Tacos are more than just a meal; they're a communal experience that fosters connections. In Guatemala's vibrant street food scene, taco stands become meeting points for friends, families, and strangers seeking sustenance and camaraderie. The act of sharing tacos brings people together, transcending boundaries and celebrating the universal language of food.

Tacos hold a special place in Guatemalan celebrations and traditions. They are often served at fiestas, birthdays, and holidays, adding a festive touch to the festivities. Their presence at these gatherings signifies not only a delicious meal but also a sense of togetherness and shared joy.

As Guatemalan cuisine continues to evolve, tacos remain a timeless favorite that stands the test of time. They serve as a bridge between generations, connecting modern-day Guatemalans to the flavors enjoyed by their ancestors. Tacos have transformed from a foreign import to a cherished culinary tradition, deeply woven into the cultural fabric of the country.

Tacos also embody the spirit of cultural exchange, a testament to the interconnectedness of global culinary traditions. Just as tacos traveled from Mexico to Guatemala, they continue to journey through time and geography, adapting and evolving with each culture they encounter. Tacos are a culinary ambassador that carries stories, flavors, and traditions from one corner of the world to another.

Guatemalan street food vendors offer a taco for every palate, catering to diverse tastes and preferences. From the carnivorous to the vegetarian, from the spice aficionado to the flavor purist, there's a taco waiting to be savored. The versatility and adaptability of tacos make them a street food treasure that transcends culinary boundaries.

Tacos invite us to embrace the joy of simple pleasures—the sizzle of the grill, the laughter of fellow diners, and the satisfaction of sinking our teeth into a well-crafted creation. Each bite is a journey through layers of flavors, a celebration of the culinary arts, and a moment of connection with the vibrant street food culture that defines Guatemala.

From humble origins to beloved street food, tacos have journeyed through time, cultures, and palates, leaving a trail of flavor and tradition in their wake. They represent more than just a convenient meal option; they encapsulate the essence of Guatemala's street food culture—a culture built on the foundation of taste, togetherness, and a passion for good food. As we savor each bite of a taco, we partake in a culinary journey that unites taste and tradition, celebrating the simple pleasures that bring joy to both locals and travelers alike.

Empanadas: Portable Pockets of Deliciousness that Define Culinary Craftsmanship

In the vibrant tapestry of Guatemalan cuisine, empanadas stand as a shining example of culinary craftsmanship—a delectable creation that marries flavors, textures, and tradition into a handheld masterpiece. These portable pockets of deliciousness, filled with a world of ingredients and culinary creativity, are more than just a snack. They are a symbol of the culinary artistry that defines street food culture in Guatemala, a testament to the country's diverse influences, and a joyful celebration of flavors that awaken the palate and warm the heart.

The empanada's journey began centuries ago, tracing its origins to medieval Spain. The word "empanada" itself comes from the Spanish verb "empanar," meaning "to coat with bread." Spanish explorers and colonizers introduced this culinary treasure to Latin America, where it took root in various countries, including Guatemala. As it traveled across oceans and continents, the empanada transformed, adapting to local ingredients and cultural preferences to become a beloved staple of street food.

At the heart of every empanada lies the shell—a delicate, flaky, and golden crust that serves as both protector and vessel. In Guatemala, empanadas often feature a masa (dough) that combines wheat flour with a touch of maize, resulting in a tender yet sturdy crust that cradles the filling within. The shell itself is a testament to the mastery of dough-making, a skill that requires precision and experience to achieve the perfect balance of crispness and softness.

What truly distinguishes empanadas is the vast array of fillings that make each bite a surprise waiting to be unraveled. From savory to sweet, Guatemalan empanadas offer a cornucopia of options that cater to every palate. Savory empanadas often showcase traditional Guatemalan flavors—chopped meats like picadillo (spiced ground meat), chorizo, and even black beans. Cheese, vegetables, and potatoes also make appearances, reflecting the country's rich culinary diversity.

The flavor profile of an empanada is elevated by the addition of spices, herbs, and condiments that add depth and complexity to the filling. A dash of cumin, a sprinkle of oregano, or a hint of garlic can transform a humble filling into a burst of flavor that dances on the palate. Salsas and sauces, whether drizzled on top or served on the side, contribute tanginess, heat, and a touch of zing that elevates the empanada experience.

Crafting an empanada is a culinary performance that requires skill and precision. The process involves a series of steps that turn raw ingredients into a pocket of delight. A portion of dough is rolled out, the filling is spooned onto the center, and then the edges are carefully folded and sealed—creating a half-moon shape that cradles the filling within. The empanada is a testament to the hands that lovingly shape each fold and seal, ensuring that the flavors remain intact with each bite.

Empanadas undergo different cooking methods, each lending its own touch to the final product. The most common methods are frying and griddling. Frying results in a crispy, golden shell that offers a satisfying crunch, while griddling creates a slightly softer and more tender crust. The choice of cooking method depends on the region, the tradition, and the desired texture.

In Guatemala's street food scene, empanadas are not just a snack; they're a culinary adventure waiting to be savored. Street vendors set up stalls on bustling corners, serving empanadas hot and fresh to hungry passersby. The experience of enjoying an empanada is a sensory journey—

the aroma of sizzling oil, the sight of the golden crust, and the anticipation of the flavors within create a moment of culinary bliss.

Empanadas have also found their way into Guatemalan cultural traditions and celebrations. They are often prepared for special occasions, fiestas, and holidays, where they serve as more than just a culinary treat. In some regions, empanadas are considered symbolic offerings, representing unity, sharing, and joy during festive gatherings.

The beauty of empanadas lies in their universal appeal—a culinary creation that transcends borders and languages. From Latin America to Europe to Asia, empanadas have found homes in diverse cultures, each adapting the recipe to suit local tastes. They serve as a testament to the interconnectedness of global cuisines and the power of food to bring people together.

For many Guatemalans, empanadas hold a special place in their hearts as comfort food— reminders of childhood, family gatherings, and simpler times. The act of enjoying an empanada often evokes feelings of nostalgia, transporting diners back to moments of warmth, joy, and togetherness.

As Guatemala's culinary landscape evolves, so do its empanadas. Creative chefs and food entrepreneurs have begun experimenting with innovative fillings that pay homage to traditional flavors while embracing modern tastes. These gourmet empanadas infuse new life into the classic snack, ensuring that its legacy continues to thrive.

From medieval Spain to the bustling streets of Guatemala, empanadas have embarked on a culinary journey that spans centuries and cultures. They have become more than just a snack; they are a testament to the craftsmanship of dough-making, the artistry of flavor combinations, and the power of food to evoke memories and emotions.

Empanadas offer a pocket of joy—a bite-sized indulgence that unites flavors, cultures, and people. Whether enjoyed on a bustling street corner or at a family gathering, each empanada is a reminder that food has the remarkable ability to transcend time and place, creating connections and leaving a lasting impression on the taste buds and the heart. As we savor the flavors of an empanada, we partake in a tradition that bridges generations, cultures, and the shared love of culinary creativity.

Tostadas: Layers of Crunch and Flavor Weaving a Culinary Tale

Amidst the lively tapestry of Guatemalan street food, one dish stands out for its vibrant colors, bold flavors, and irresistible textures—tostadas. These culinary creations are more than just a meal; they're a work of art that weaves together layers of crunch and flavor in a symphony that dances on the palate. From the initial crack of the crispy tortilla to the explosion of taste from the toppings, tostadas embody the essence of Guatemalan street food—a celebration of tradition, creativity, and the joy of indulging in a culinary masterpiece.

Tostadas have ancient roots that stretch far back in culinary history. The concept of a toasted or fried tortilla topped with ingredients has been a part of various cultures across Latin America for centuries. In Guatemala, tostadas have evolved to become a cherished street food, a canvas for culinary exploration that brings together diverse flavors and textures in one delectable bite.

At the heart of every tostada lies the star of the show—the tostada shell itself. Crafted from corn tortillas, the shells are meticulously prepared to achieve the perfect balance of crispiness and resilience. Whether by frying, griddling, or baking, the tortillas are transformed into golden, crunchy canvases that provide a sturdy foundation for the layers of toppings to come.

What sets tostadas apart is the artful layering of toppings that creates a visually stunning and incredibly flavorful dish. The possibilities are endless, offering a wide range of ingredients that reflect Guatemala's rich culinary heritage. Refried beans, shredded lettuce, diced tomatoes, crumbled cheese, and minced meats such as chicken, pork, or beef are common choices. But the beauty of tostadas lies in the freedom to mix and match, allowing every vendor and diner to put their unique twist on this beloved dish.

The tostada experience would be incomplete without the vibrant salsas and sauces that amplify the flavor profile. Salsa roja and salsa verde, made from a medley of tomatoes, chili peppers, onions, and herbs, infuse each bite with a burst of tanginess and heat. Creamy avocado sauce, drizzles of lime juice, and dollops of crema add layers of creaminess and brightness that balance the richness of the toppings.

Tostadas are a masterclass in texture play—a delightful dance of contrasts that elevates the eating experience. The crunch of the tostada shell gives way to the tender beans, the juicy tomatoes, and the creamy cheese. Each bite is a celebration of the harmonious interplay between crisp and soft, creating a sensory symphony that captivates the taste buds.

Crafting a tostada is akin to a choreographed dance—a sequence of movements that results in a beautiful, delicious creation. The tostada shell is carefully placed on the plate, a canvas ready to be adorned. The layers of ingredients are added with precision—a spoonful of beans here, a handful of lettuce there, a scattering of cheese, and a flourish of salsa. The final result is a visual masterpiece that begs to be savored.

Tostadas transcend mere sustenance; they are a canvas that captures the essence of Guatemalan culture. Each layer represents a piece of the country's history, a reflection of its indigenous heritage and its culinary fusion with Spanish and other influences. The tostada's versatility allows it to accommodate local ingredients, transforming it into a dish that speaks to Guatemala's diverse regions and tastes.

Tostadas have also earned their place as centerpieces during cultural celebrations and family gatherings. From birthdays to religious festivals, tostadas grace tables with their colorful presentation and bold flavors. They are shared among loved ones, symbolizing unity and togetherness—a testament to the role food plays in fostering connections and building memories.

While tostadas are beloved street food classics, they've also ventured into the realm of gourmet cuisine. Innovative chefs and culinary enthusiasts have taken tostadas to new heights by experimenting with unconventional toppings and creative presentations. This evolution ensures that the dish remains a timeless favorite while also embracing contemporary tastes.

Indulging in a tostada is not just about satisfying hunger; it's about experiencing a feast for the senses. The aroma of freshly fried tortillas, the visual allure of colorful toppings, the satisfying crunch as you take the first bite—every element adds to the joy of the culinary journey. Tostadas invite you to savor each moment, to appreciate the craftsmanship, and to immerse yourself in a sensory adventure.

From the ancient traditions of indigenous cultures to the bustling streets of modern Guatemala, tostadas have woven a culinary legacy that transcends time and geography. They are a tribute to the art of layering flavors, a nod to the cultural diversity that defines Guatemala, and a reminder that simple ingredients can be transformed into something extraordinary.

Tostadas offer more than just a meal; they offer a flavorful encounter with tradition, innovation, and the rich tapestry of Guatemalan cuisine. With each bite, you embark on a culinary journey that travels through history and culture, inviting you to explore the layers of crunch and flavor that make tostadas a cherished emblem of street food culture.

Elote Loco: Grilled Corn Magic That Ignites the Senses

In the bustling streets of Guatemala, an intoxicating aroma mingles with the sounds of laughter and the sights of vibrant colors. The source of this olfactory symphony? Elote Loco, a street food sensation that captures the essence of Guatemalan street culture—a celebration of flavors, creativity, and the joy of indulging in a simple yet irresistible delight. Elote Loco, or "Crazy Corn," is not just a snack; it's a sensory experience that ignites the taste buds, warms the heart, and leaves a lasting memory of the magic that can be conjured from the simplest of ingredients.

Elote Loco's origins can be traced to the tradition of street corn found in many parts of the world. From Mexico's "elote" to Central American variations, this beloved treat has traversed borders and cultures, adapting to local tastes and ingredients along the way. In Guatemala, elote has found its own unique twist, earning its "loco" title through the addition of flavorful toppings that transform a simple cob of corn into a culinary masterpiece.

At the heart of Elote Loco lies the humble cob of corn—an ingredient that, with a little culinary magic, becomes a canvas for creativity. The corn is grilled to perfection, allowing its natural sweetness to intensify and infuse each kernel with a smoky essence. The grilling process caramelizes the sugars in the corn, creating a symphony of flavors that are released with every bite.

What sets Elote Loco apart is its array of toppings that add depth, complexity, and a touch of "locura" (craziness) to the dish. A generous slather of mayonnaise, a sprinkle of crumbled cheese—often cotija or queso fresco—and a dusting of chili powder or Tajín provide a medley of textures and flavors. The combination of creamy, tangy, and spicy elements creates a harmonious blend that dances on the taste buds.

Elote Loco encapsulates the spirit of cultural fusion—an emblem of how culinary traditions can merge and evolve. While it has its roots in Central American street food culture, it also pays homage to the influence of Mexican cuisine, with its use of chili powder and cheese. This fusion of flavors adds a layer of complexity that transcends borders and brings people together.

The creation of Elote Loco is an art form in itself—a careful process that requires attention to detail and a passion for presentation. A skewer is inserted into the grilled corn, serving as both a handle and a means of dipping the cob into the toppings. The layering of ingredients— mayonnaise, cheese, chili powder, and sometimes lime juice—requires a deft hand to ensure that each element is evenly distributed and adheres to the cob.

Elote Loco's visual appeal is a feast for the eyes—a riot of colors and textures that beckon passersby to partake in its deliciousness. The cob of corn, glistening with grill marks, contrasts with the creamy mayonnaise and the vibrant hues of the chili powder. The crumbled cheese adds an artistic touch, creating a dish that's as delightful to behold as it is to devour.

Elote Loco has become synonymous with festive gatherings and celebrations in Guatemala. From street fairs to religious festivals, it graces tables and street corners, offering a burst of flavor and a sense of camaraderie. Its presence at these events serves as a reminder that food is not just nourishment; it's a way of sharing joy, connecting with others, and celebrating life's moments.

For many Guatemalans, Elote Loco evokes feelings of nostalgia—a reminder of childhood memories, family outings, and carefree moments. The act of enjoying an elote elicits emotions tied to comfort, familiarity, and a connection to tradition. It's a food that transcends generations, uniting grandparents, parents, and children through the simple act of savoring a cob of corn.

In Guatemala's vibrant street food scene, Elote Loco takes center stage as a culinary theater in itself. Street vendors set up their stalls, grilling corn to perfection and crafting each elote with care. The sizzle of the grill, the assembly of toppings, and the interactions between vendors and customers create a sensory experience that's as much about community as it is about food.

As Guatemala's culinary landscape evolves, Elote Loco is not immune to innovation. Chefs and food enthusiasts have taken this classic street food to new heights, experimenting with unconventional toppings, gourmet variations, and creative presentations. These modern twists on Elote Loco ensure that its legacy remains alive while also embracing contemporary tastes.

From its humble beginnings as a simple cob of corn to its status as a beloved street food icon, Elote Loco has embarked on a culinary journey that spans time, cultures, and palates. It captures the essence of Guatemalan street food culture—a celebration of flavor, creativity, and the joy of indulging in a treat that's both humble and extraordinary.

Indulging in an Elote Loco is more than just savoring a delicious dish; it's embracing a sensory journey that awakens the taste buds, nourishes the soul, and fosters a connection with the community. The smoky aroma, the creamy texture, the burst of tanginess and heat—all contribute to an experience that's both fleeting and enduring. As you take that first bite of Elote Loco, you partake in a culinary magic that transcends the cob of corn, touching hearts and igniting the senses in a celebration of flavor, culture, and the art of street food.

Rellenitos: Sweet and Savory Indulgence Weaving Flavors and Traditions

In the vibrant culinary tapestry of Guatemala, a unique treat stands out for its harmonious blend of flavors, textures, and cultural significance—rellenitos. These delectable morsels encapsulate the essence of Guatemalan street food culture, inviting both locals and visitors to indulge in a sweet and savory journey that weaves tradition, creativity, and the joy of savoring a cherished emblem of the country's culinary heritage.

Rellenitos have their roots in Guatemala's rich culinary history, drawing inspiration from the traditional dish "rellenos," which translates to "stuffed." This dish typically features mashed plantains stuffed with black beans and then fried. Over time, the concept evolved into rellenitos, a culinary innovation that added a touch of sweetness to the traditional recipe.

At the heart of rellenitos lies the star ingredient—ripe plantains. These starchy fruits, beloved across Central America, offer a subtle sweetness and a tender texture that make them ideal for both savory and sweet applications. Rellenitos highlight the plantain's versatility, transforming it from an unassuming ingredient into a canvas for culinary creativity.

Crafting rellenitos requires culinary craftsmanship and attention to detail. The process begins with the plantains, which are boiled until tender, then mashed to a smooth consistency. The sweet and savory magic happens when the mashed plantains are enveloped around a core of refried black beans. This stuffing creates a delightful contrast of flavors and textures that defines rellenitos.

Once the rellenitos are carefully assembled, they're fried to perfection—a culinary transformation that brings out the best in both the sweet and savory elements. The outer layer of the rellenitos becomes irresistibly crisp, creating a textural symphony that is at once crunchy and soft, tender and slightly caramelized.

What truly sets rellenitos apart is their dual nature—a sweet and savory profile that intertwines to create a harmonious indulgence. The rich, earthy flavors of the refried black beans are complemented by the natural sweetness of the plantains. This balance is a testament to the culinary ingenuity that defines Guatemalan cuisine, where unexpected flavor pairings create unforgettable taste experiences.

Rellenitos hold cultural significance beyond their culinary allure. They provide a window into Guatemala's indigenous heritage, where food is often a bridge between generations and a reflection of ancestral traditions. Rellenitos' presence in street food culture serves as a reminder

of the importance of preserving and celebrating the flavors and customs that shape the country's identity.

Rellenitos have earned their place as beloved street food classics in Guatemala's bustling culinary scene. Street vendors set up their stalls, offering locals and tourists alike the opportunity to experience the delight of rellenitos on the go. The act of purchasing a warm rellenito from a vendor's cart adds a sense of authenticity to the culinary journey, connecting you to the pulse of street food culture.

While traditional rellenitos remain a favorite, Guatemala's evolving culinary landscape has paved the way for creative interpretations. Some vendors experiment with variations, introducing new fillings, such as chocolate or caramelized bananas, that add an extra layer of sweetness to the dish. These innovative twists honor the classic while also embracing contemporary tastes.

Rellenitos often make appearances at festive gatherings and special occasions. From birthdays to holidays, they grace tables with their flavorful presence, symbolizing unity, sharing, and the joy of celebration. The act of enjoying a rellenito becomes a culinary tradition in itself—a way of honoring culture, family, and community.

Rellenitos embody Guatemala's culinary heritage—a legacy passed down through generations. As you savor each bite, you partake in a journey that transcends time and borders, connecting you to the traditions, flavors, and stories that have shaped the country's identity.

Indulging in rellenitos is more than just enjoying a snack; it's savoring a sweet and savory symphony that resonates on the palate and in the heart. The melding of flavors, the contrasts of textures, and the cultural significance all contribute to an experience that transcends the plate. Rellenitos invite you to embrace tradition, celebrate innovation, and immerse yourself in the joy of savoring a culinary treasure that defines Guatemalan street food culture.

Pupusas: A Taste of Tradition Weaving the Flavors of El Salvador

In the heart of El Salvador's culinary heritage lies a beloved dish that embodies the essence of tradition, community, and the art of savoring simple pleasures—pupusas. These delectable treats, considered a national treasure, are more than just a meal; they're a culinary journey that transports both locals and visitors to the heart of El Salvador's cultural tapestry. With their

humble origins, rich flavors, and communal significance, pupusas have captured the hearts and palates of those who seek an authentic taste of El Salvador.

The history of pupusas can be traced back hundreds of years, to the indigenous Pipil people of what is now El Salvador. These ancient cultures combined cornmeal with various fillings to create a satisfying and portable dish that could sustain them during their daily activities. Pupusas, then and now, represent more than just nourishment; they symbolize the resilience and resourcefulness of the people who created them.

At the core of every pupusa lies maize—a staple crop that has been the backbone of Central American cuisine for centuries. Cornmeal masa, made from ground maize, is the foundation of pupusas, providing a canvas that's both pliable and sturdy. The art of crafting pupusas begins with the hands that lovingly shape the masa, infusing each pupusa with a touch of warmth and tradition.

What truly sets pupusas apart is the diverse array of fillings that elevate them from simple dough pockets to flavorful masterpieces. While cheese and beans are classic choices, pupusas can be filled with an endless variety of ingredients—pork, chicken, loroco (an edible flower bud), and even shrimp, to name a few. These fillings create a symphony of flavors that capture the essence of El Salvador's culinary landscape.

Crafting pupusas is a culinary craft that requires precision, patience, and an appreciation for tradition. The process involves taking a small portion of masa, shaping it into a thin disk, adding the chosen filling, and then sealing the edges to create a pocket. The pupusas are then cooked on a griddle, where the outer layer of masa transforms into a golden, slightly crispy shell that encases the flavorful filling within.

Pupusas are often accompanied by a symphony of salsas that elevate the flavors and add an extra layer of vibrancy. Curtido, a fermented cabbage slaw, provides a tangy and refreshing contrast to the richness of the pupusas. Salsa roja and salsa verde, made from chili peppers and other ingredients, contribute a burst of heat and zest that awaken the taste buds.

Beyond their culinary appeal, pupusas hold cultural significance as a symbol of community and connection. Pupuserías, small restaurants or stands specializing in pupusas, are gathering places where people from all walks of life come together to share a meal and create lasting memories. Pupusas are a reminder that food has the power to foster connections, celebrate tradition, and bring people closer.

Pupusas take center stage during festive occasions, celebrations, and family gatherings in El Salvador. From birthdays to holidays, pupusas are a culinary highlight that graces tables with their comforting presence. They evoke a sense of comfort, nostalgia, and togetherness, as family and friends come together to indulge in the simple joy of savoring this cherished dish.

The art of making pupusas is often passed down through generations, from grandmothers to mothers to daughters, creating a sense of continuity and connection. The act of teaching and learning to make pupusas is a reflection of the cultural values of sharing and preserving tradition, ensuring that the artistry of pupusa-making remains alive and thriving.

In El Salvador, pupusas are ubiquitous street food, enjoyed by locals and sought after by visitors eager to experience an authentic taste of the country. Pupusa vendors set up their stalls on street corners and marketplaces, creating a sensory experience that tantalizes passersby with the aroma of sizzling masa and flavorful fillings. The sight of pupusas cooking on the griddle and the sound of the sizzle create an irresistible invitation to indulge.

While pupusas remain a cherished tradition, they've also embraced culinary innovation. Creative chefs and culinary enthusiasts have experimented with unique fillings, modern presentations, and gourmet interpretations of the classic dish. This evolution ensures that pupusas remain a beloved staple while also appealing to contemporary tastes.

Pupusas are more than just a dish; they're a culinary legacy that encapsulates the heart and soul of El Salvador. With each bite, you partake in a journey through time, culture, and tradition, connecting you to the stories, flavors, and spirit of a country that values community, family, and the simple pleasure of sharing a meal.

Indulging in a pupusa is not just about satisfying hunger; it's about embracing a taste of tradition, experiencing the warmth of community, and celebrating the art of simplicity. The textures, flavors, and cultural significance woven into each pupusa create a sensory experience that transcends the plate, inviting you to savor the essence of El Salvador and the time-honored joy of enjoying a meal that embodies the heart and soul of a nation.

Chuchitos: Guatemala's Tamale Delights Weaving Tradition and Flavor

In the heart of Guatemala's culinary landscape, a beloved dish holds the spotlight, captivating both locals and visitors with its rich flavors and cultural significance—chuchitos. These delectable treats, often referred to as Guatemala's answer to tamales, embody the essence of tradition, history, and the art of savoring a dish that has woven its way into the fabric of Guatemalan culture. With their humble origins, diverse fillings, and the warmth of community, chuchitos offer a taste of Guatemala's soul and a culinary journey that is as inviting as it is unforgettable.

Chuchitos have a history as rich and varied as the country they hail from. The concept of wrapped food—a precursor to tamales and chuchitos—can be traced back to ancient Mesoamerican cultures. These cultures combined masa (corn dough) with various fillings to create portable and nourishing meals. Over time, this culinary tradition evolved into the beloved dish we know as chuchitos today, a testament to the enduring legacy of Guatemalan cuisine.

At the heart of every chuchito lies the essence of the dish—masa. Masa, made from ground corn that's been soaked, cooked, and ground into a smooth dough, serves as the vessel that holds together the flavors within. The masa's pliability allows for the expert craftsmanship of chuchitos, where hands shape, fill, and fold each delicate package with care and precision.

What truly sets chuchitos apart is the diversity of fillings that grace their interiors. While tamales may be more commonly associated with meat fillings, chuchitos offer a wider variety of options. From chicken and beef to vegetables and cheeses, the fillings are as varied as Guatemala's landscapes. This variety speaks to the country's rich culinary heritage and its fusion of indigenous, Spanish, and other cultural influences.

Creating chuchitos is a culinary art form that requires both skill and patience. The process begins with a dollop of masa, which is expertly shaped and pressed into a flat surface. A spoonful of filling is placed in the center, and the masa is folded and sealed to create a neat package. The result is a pocket of goodness that encapsulates the flavors and traditions of Guatemala.

Traditionally, chuchitos are wrapped in a square of dried corn husk, creating a charming presentation reminiscent of a gift waiting to be unwrapped. The husk not only imparts a subtle corn flavor to the masa but also allows the chuchito to steam to perfection, resulting in a tender and flavorful bite.

Chuchitos are typically steamed to perfection, allowing the flavors of the masa and fillings to meld together in a symphony of taste. The steaming process transforms the masa into a delicate, moist texture, while also infusing the fillings with the subtle aroma of the corn husk. The result is a dish that's both comforting and indulgent, capturing the essence of Guatemalan comfort food.

Beyond their culinary appeal, chuchitos hold a special place in Guatemalan culture as a symbol of connection and community. Chuchiterías, the small stands or shops that specialize in chuchitos, become gathering places where people from all walks of life come together to enjoy a meal. The act of sharing chuchitos fosters a sense of camaraderie, reminding us of the power of food to bring people closer.

Chuchitos are often enjoyed during celebrations, holidays, and special occasions in Guatemala. From birthdays to religious festivals, they grace tables with their presence, offering a burst of

flavor and a sense of tradition. They evoke a sense of nostalgia, creating a bridge between generations as families come together to enjoy a dish that has stood the test of time.

The art of making chuchitos is often passed down through generations, from grandmothers to mothers to daughters. This passing down of knowledge is a testament to the importance of preserving heritage and culinary traditions. As young and old gather in kitchens to shape masa, fill chuchitos, and share stories, the essence of Guatemala's culinary history lives on.

In Guatemala's vibrant street food scene, chuchitos have earned their place as beloved classics. Street vendors set up their stalls, expertly crafting chuchitos to order. The sight of chuchitos being wrapped, the sounds of bustling activity, and the aroma of steaming masa create a sensory experience that's as much about culture as it is about food.

While chuchitos remain rooted in tradition, they've also embraced culinary innovation. Creative chefs and food enthusiasts have experimented with modern interpretations, introducing unique fillings, flavors, and presentations that honor the classic while also appealing to contemporary tastes.

Chuchitos are more than just a dish; they're a culinary legacy that embodies the heart and soul of Guatemala. With each bite, you partake in a journey through time, culture, and flavor, connecting you to the stories, traditions, and spirit of a country that values community, family, and the art of savoring a meal.

Indulging in chuchitos is more than just enjoying a snack; it's savoring a piece of history, experiencing the warmth of tradition, and celebrating the culinary craft that has brought joy to generations. The layers of masa, the diversity of fillings, and the cultural significance all contribute to an experience that transcends the plate, inviting you to savor the heart and soul of Guatemala's culinary heritage.

Bocadillos: Sweet Bites of Guilty Pleasure Weaving Delight and Tradition

In the realm of Guatemalan confections, a treat of undeniable charm and temptation reigns supreme—bocadillos. These delightful morsels, known as "little bites" in Spanish, capture the essence of Guatemalan sweetness, tradition, and the simple joy of indulging in a guilty pleasure. With their humble origins, sugary allure, and cultural significance, bocadillos offer a delectable glimpse into Guatemala's culinary soul, inviting all who partake to savor the sweetness of life.

Bocadillos have been enchanting Guatemalan palates for generations, tracing their origins back to the heart of the country's culinary traditions. Rooted in simplicity, bocadillos emerged as an ingenious way to transform everyday ingredients into delightful treats. As the years have passed, these sweet bites have woven themselves into the fabric of Guatemalan culture, becoming a beloved emblem of homemade goodness.

At the core of every bocadillo is a simple but essential ingredient—panela. Panela, also known as piloncillo or rapadura, is an unrefined sugar that is derived from sugarcane. With its rich, caramel-like flavor and deep golden hue, panela becomes the sweet foundation upon which bocadillos are built. This natural sweetness is a testament to the beauty of working with raw ingredients that carry the essence of the land.

The art of crafting bocadillos is a labor of love—a culinary endeavor that demands patience, attention, and a respect for tradition. The process begins with the dissolution of panela in water, creating a syrup that serves as the base for the bocadillo mixture. The syrup is then cooked and stirred until it reaches a precise consistency, at which point it's skillfully poured into molds to set.

While panela takes center stage, bocadillos delight in exploring a world of flavors. From the classic panela bocadillos to variations enriched with ingredients like coconut, nuts, and fruits, the array of options ensures that there's a bocadillo to satisfy every palate. This versatility reflects the spirit of Guatemalan cuisine, where tradition and innovation harmoniously coexist.

Bocadillos are intricately woven into Guatemalan traditions, often gracing tables during celebrations, holidays, and special occasions. From Christmas to religious festivities, bocadillos become a culinary highlight that brings a touch of sweetness to the festivities. These treats are a reminder that food is not just sustenance; it's a way of celebrating life's moments and sharing joy with loved ones.

Beyond their culinary appeal, bocadillos hold cultural significance as a symbol of community and connection. In Guatemalan markets and street corners, vendors expertly craft and sell bocadillos, creating spaces where people gather to indulge in a shared love for these sweet bites. The act of enjoying a bocadillo fosters a sense of camaraderie, underscoring the power of food to bring people together.

While bocadillos are undoubtedly linked to special occasions, they also find their place in the rhythm of daily life. Whether enjoyed as an afternoon snack, a treat to satisfy a sweet tooth, or a nostalgic homage to childhood, bocadillos bring a touch of simple pleasure to the mundane. They offer a reminder that life's sweetness can be savored in the everyday moments.

The craftsmanship that goes into creating bocadillos is not limited to their flavor; it extends to their visual presentation. Bocadillos are often molded into intricate shapes that are as much a

feast for the eyes as they are for the palate. From delicate flowers to whimsical animals, each bocadillo is a miniature work of art that reflects the care and creativity invested in their making.

Indulging in bocadillos is more than just savoring a sweet treat; it's embarking on a sensory journey that connects you to the flavors, traditions, and warmth of Guatemalan culture. The rich, caramel notes of panela, the textures that melt in your mouth, and the moments of pure enjoyment—all contribute to an experience that transcends the plate.

In Guatemala's vibrant street food culture, bocadillos find their place among the array of tempting delights. Street vendors expertly display and sell bocadillos, inviting passersby to indulge in a taste of this beloved treat. The sight of the golden bites and the aroma of panela create an irresistible invitation, making it impossible to resist the allure of bocadillos.

For many Guatemalans, bocadillos evoke feelings of nostalgia, warmth, and comfort. The act of enjoying a bocadillo can transport them back to simpler times, to memories of childhood and the flavors of home. Bocadillos are a reminder that food is not just sustenance; it's a vessel for emotions, a connection to one's roots, and a celebration of culture.

Bocadillos are more than just sweet bites; they're a culinary treasure that encapsulates the heart and soul of Guatemala. With each bite, you partake in a journey that transcends time, flavors, and experiences, connecting you to the stories, traditions, and sweetness that define the country's culinary landscape.

Indulging in a bocadillo is more than just savoring a confection; it's embracing a taste of tradition, experiencing the joy of community, and celebrating the simple pleasure of a treat that speaks to the heart. The flavors, the memories, and the cultural significance woven into each bocadillo create a sensory experience that transcends the plate, inviting you to savor the sweetness of life itself.

Chapines and Guatemalan Delights: A Culinary Adventure

In the heart of Central America, a country known for its diverse landscapes, vibrant culture, and rich history, lies a culinary journey waiting to be explored. Guatemala, often referred to as the "Land of Eternal Spring," is a treasure trove of flavors, traditions, and delights that beckon both locals and visitors to savor its culinary offerings. At the center of this gastronomic adventure are the people themselves, known as "chapines," whose passion for food and the art of savoring

life's pleasures has given rise to a tapestry of Guatemalan delights that reflect the country's cultural tapestry and culinary ingenuity.

The term "chapines" is a colloquial term used to refer to Guatemalan people, capturing the essence of their identity and culture. The people of Guatemala, diverse in their heritage and traditions, share a common thread—their deep appreciation for the joys of life, especially when it comes to food. Whether it's a simple street snack or a festive feast, chapines embrace the act of eating as an opportunity to connect, celebrate, and savor the flavors that make their country unique.

Guatemalan cuisine is a reflection of the country's history, geography, and cultural influences. It weaves together indigenous traditions, Spanish colonial legacies, and modern innovations to create a culinary symphony that is as diverse as the country itself. From the highlands to the lowlands, each region contributes its own ingredients, techniques, and flavors, resulting in a dynamic culinary landscape that caters to every palate.

Guatemalan culinary traditions are deeply rooted in the country's history and indigenous heritage. The use of native ingredients such as maize, beans, and chilies pays homage to the ancestral practices that have shaped the country's cuisine for centuries. From the preparation of traditional tamales to the crafting of artisanal chocolate, every culinary tradition tells a story of resilience, resourcefulness, and the beauty of preserving heritage.

In Guatemala, street food culture is a vibrant tapestry that brings people together through the shared love of food. Chapines and visitors alike indulge in the pleasures of street food, where small stalls and carts offer a taste of the country's culinary treasures. Whether it's enjoying a plate of crispy tostadas piled high with toppings, or savoring the warmth of a freshly made pupusa, street food becomes a window into the heart of Guatemala's everyday life.

Local markets, bustling with energy and colors, are a culinary playground where chapines and travelers can explore the bounty of Guatemala's ingredients. Vendors proudly display fresh fruits, vegetables, spices, and more, inviting visitors to engage in a sensory experience that celebrates the beauty of local produce. These markets are a testament to the country's agricultural richness and the close connection between people and the land.

Guatemalan culture places a strong emphasis on communal gatherings and celebrations, many of which are centered around food. From the vibrant Día de los Muertos (Day of the Dead) festivities to the joyful Feria de Jocotenango, food takes center stage as families and communities come together to share in the abundance of the season. These feasts are a testament to the deep connection between food and the spirit of celebration.

Guatemala's diverse geography—from volcanic highlands to coastal shores—means that its culinary offerings are rich and varied. Ingredients such as avocado, chayote, and squash find their way into hearty stews, while the abundance of seafood graces plates with dishes that

capture the flavors of the ocean. From the comforting caldo de res (beef soup) to the zesty ceviche, every bite tells a story of the country's connection to its natural surroundings.

Guatemala's sweet offerings are equally enchanting, showcasing the country's talent for creating sugary delights that captivate the palate. From the iconic tres leches cake, drenched in three types of milk, to the rich and velvety chocolate atole, these desserts offer a satisfying conclusion to any meal. The art of crafting bocadillos and other sweet treats underscores Guatemala's knack for infusing every bite with a touch of sweetness and tradition.

Guatemala is renowned for its exceptional coffee, which has become a global ambassador for the country's agricultural prowess. The high-altitude regions provide the ideal conditions for cultivating beans with nuanced flavors and distinct profiles. A cup of Guatemalan coffee is not just a beverage; it's a sensory experience that invites you to savor the nuances of each sip and appreciate the meticulous process that brings this elixir to life.

Chapines take great pride in preserving their culinary heritage and passing down traditional recipes from generation to generation. Family kitchens become classrooms, where grandparents teach their grandchildren the art of crafting tamales or forming pupusas. This passing down of knowledge ensures that Guatemalan culinary traditions remain alive and vibrant, creating a bridge between the past and the present.

In every corner of Guatemala, whether it's the bustling streets of Guatemala City or the tranquil landscapes of Lake Atitlán, the spirit of chapines and the allure of Guatemalan delights can be felt. The flavors, the traditions, and the warmth of connection that define the country's culinary culture invite you to embark on a journey of tastes and experiences that unveil the heart and soul of Guatemala.

Indulging in Guatemalan delights is not just about satisfying hunger; it's about embracing the joys of life and celebrating a culture that thrives on the pleasures of food and community. With each bite of a tamale, each sip of coffee, and each shared meal, you partake in a sensory experience that transcends the plate and immerses you in the essence of Guatemala—a country where every flavor tells a story, and every dish is a celebration of life itself.

Conclusion: Embarking on a Culinary Odyssey Through Guatemala's Delights

As we conclude our exploration of Guatemala's culinary landscape, we find ourselves immersed in a tapestry of flavors, traditions, and stories that have woven themselves into the heart and soul of the country. From the bustling streets of Guatemala City to the tranquil shores of Lake Atitlán, from the highland markets to the vibrant celebrations, the essence of Guatemalan cuisine reflects the rich history, diverse culture, and vibrant spirit of its people.

Guatemala's culinary journey is a captivating blend of indigenous roots, Spanish colonial influences, and contemporary innovations. This convergence of cultures and flavors creates a diverse and dynamic gastronomic tapestry that celebrates the country's history and heritage. Each bite tells a story of the past and the present, inviting us to explore the intricate layers of tradition and modernity that define Guatemalan cuisine.

From the hearty stews and savory tamales to the sweet bocadillos and artisanal chocolates, Guatemalan cuisine is a reflection of the country's identity and the people's deep connection to their land. The use of native ingredients, such as maize, beans, and chilies, pays homage to the culinary practices of indigenous communities that have flourished for centuries. These traditions are not just recipes; they're a testament to the resilience and creativity of a people who have shaped their cuisine through generations.

Guatemala's culinary culture is deeply rooted in the spirit of community and celebration. Whether it's a lively fiesta, a family gathering, or a street food market, food serves as a focal point for bringing people together. The act of sharing a meal becomes an opportunity to connect, bond, and celebrate the joys of life. Guatemalan cuisine, in all its forms, is a reminder of the power of food to foster connections and create lasting memories.

The diverse landscapes of Guatemala provide the canvas upon which its culinary traditions are painted. From the highlands to the lowlands, from the volcanic terrain to the coastal shores, each region contributes its unique ingredients and culinary techniques. The bounty of fresh produce, seafood, and traditional staples infuses each dish with a sense of place, allowing us to taste the flavors of Guatemala's natural surroundings.

Throughout our journey, we've witnessed the importance of passing down culinary traditions from one generation to the next. The art of making tamales, crafting pupusas, and creating bocadillos is not just about the act itself; it's about preserving a heritage that speaks to the

essence of Guatemalan culture. In family kitchens and local markets, the flame of tradition continues to burn bright, ensuring that the flavors of the past remain a vital part of the present.

As we take our final steps on this culinary odyssey through Guatemala's delights, we are reminded of the simple pleasure of savoring life's joys. Whether it's indulging in a plate of tamales, enjoying a cup of aromatic coffee, or relishing the sweetness of bocadillos, every taste is an invitation to immerse ourselves fully in the present moment. Guatemalan cuisine teaches us that food is more than sustenance; it's a vessel for connection, culture, and celebration.

Our exploration of Guatemalan cuisine is a testament to the country's rich cultural heritage and the vibrant spirit of its people. It's an invitation to explore the hidden gems of street food stalls, uncover the secrets of traditional markets, and embrace the flavors that define a nation. From the bustling cities to the serene landscapes, every corner of Guatemala offers a culinary adventure waiting to be savored.

In the end, our journey through Guatemala's culinary delights has been a celebration of culture, community, and the art of savoring life's pleasures. The flavors we've tasted, the traditions we've encountered, and the stories we've uncovered have left an indelible mark, reminding us that food is a universal language that brings us all together, no matter our backgrounds or borders. So, let's continue to explore, embrace, and share the joys of Guatemalan cuisine and the culinary treasures that await us around the world.

Printed in Great Britain
by Amazon

36188181R00073